George Columbus Williams

The Rights of the People in Money

George Columbus Williams

The Rights of the People in Money

ISBN/EAN: 9783744736299

Printed in Europe, USA, Canada, Australia, Japan

Cover: Foto ©Suzi / pixelio.de

More available books at **www.hansebooks.com**

THE

RIGHTS OF THE PEOPLE

IN

MONEY.

BY GEORGE WILLIAMS.

TOLEDO, OHIO:
BLADE PRINTING & PAPER COMPANY,
1876

PREFACE.

THE RIGHTS OF THE PEOPLE IN MONEY.

This book was written to announce and maintain the principle that money is entirely a public thing, chosen by society and made and legalized by government as an authoritative standard of value and medium of exchange in the affairs of the government and people. That the custom of society and law of government make it necessary for the individual members of society to procure and use it in their business affairs and to pay taxes and public revenues. And hence that every member of society and subject of the government has *a right* to meet money in business, in exchange for property, services, or labor; subject to the choice of the holders to make the exchange, and also subject to the competition that other people's property, ser-

vices, or labor may offer for it; but not subject to any right in the holders to make gain
out of it, while they refuse to make such exchange, nor while by notes and promises to pay
money they hold it bound to return to themselves, excepting only the money invested in
the bonds and promises to pay of the United
States Government. That it is the duty of
the government to protect these common
rights in the money by sufficient penalties
and confiscations of property and money involved in violating them in any form, especially in the form that is generally known as
lending money for interest, or in exchanging
it for private promise to pay money.

It is not the intention to give a scientific
treatise on money, but to illustrate the common rights in it, and note and refute the
sophisms of lending money for interest as
they come up in the mind from the pages of
fourty-four years of business experience, or
as they are suggested by current events.
There will be copious quotations from the
works of learned authors and from lectures
and newspaper articles to show the tendency

and direction of the learning of the world on the subject of money, with such comments on the same as may help to let the truth appear over all. It will be the especial effort to make every chapter and article as near as possible a complete argument in itself against lending money for interest.

GEORGE WILLIAMS.

Northwood, Columbus, Ohio.

CONTENTS.

THE

RIGHTS OF THE PEOPLE IN MONEY

CHAPTER I.

The bankers and money-lenders are rapidly breaking up the business of the country, are taking the property from the mass of the people, and are reducing them to a condition of hopeless poverty and degradation. To understand the power for evil that the bankers and money-lenders are exercising over the mass of the people by means of the money, it is necessary to revert to first principles and consider

WHAT MONEY IS AND WHAT IT IS FOR.

Money is a sign of value, and a medium of exchanging value, adopted by custom in the transaction of business, and legalized by government, and made a final end or test of value that labor and property, and other things of value, shall be referred to and valued by. The affairs of civilized society and government require the presence of a universal sign or representative of value, that real values shall be made to end or terminate in.

The ending of all value in money, is effected by custom and law, making a constant necessity for labor and property, to be converted into money to pay taxes and public revenues, and also business balances, at the option of creditors. This constant exchange of labor and property for money is necessary in the affairs both of the government and of the people, in securing and maintaining an interchangeable relation between money and labor and property. In a primitive state of society,

THE ESSENTIAL FEATURES OF MONEY

could only be secured by making it of gold and silver. These metals are but little subject to waste by rust, and as they exist in limited supply, it is supposed to cost as much in labor to procure them, as it would to pro-

cure the things that they are the price of
But whatever money may be made of, the controlling powers above enumerated must be
organized in it by custom or law, or by both.
These essential and controlling powers in
money, afford the opportunity for the holders
of it to inflict upon all the rest of the people
the most terrible oppression and abject servitude, if they are not restrained by the power
that makes the money.   As is now seen, custom and law lay a necessity upon the people,
to determine and end all value in money, and
this requires of them to constantly procure
and use money; a thing impossible for them
to do, unless they can get it in exchange for
labor and property.   Now, the bankers and
money-lenders, having gotten the money in
exchange for labor and property, refuse to let
other people get it in that way, but hold it
until the need resting upon the people to pay
business balances and public revenues, will
compel them to borrow the money on promises for its return to the lenders with increase.
The light of common reason, as well as sore
experience, clearly shows that it is not possi-

ble for the people to fulfill the conditions made for them now, by the joint action of the government and the bankers and money-lenders, and that the bankers and money-lenders will continue, as they are doing now, to break up the business of the country, and take the property from the mass of the people, until they take all the property, and reduce all the laborers to a condition of abject poverty and servitude; or until the government, the money-making power, restrains the evil business of money lending.

As the individual members of society are placed under the necessity to procure and use money, by a regulation of society and government, to the intent that they shall be compelled to constantly exchange labor and property for money, and thereby establish and maintain an interchangeable relation between money and labor and property for the benefit of society and government, there results

THE RIGHT TO EVERY MEMBER OF SOCIETY

to meet money in worldly affairs in exchange for labor and property, subject to the choice of the holders of the money to make the exchange, and also subject to the competition that other people's labor or property may offer for it; but not subject to any right in the holders to make gain, while they refuse to exchange it for labor or property, nor while by notes and promises to pay money, they hold it bound to be returned to themselves.

The right to meet money in worldly affairs to be exchanged for labor and property without any right for holders to make gain while they hold it back from such exchange, is as important to the individual as his right to liberty; for it is evident that his liberty and his condition will depend upon this right in money.

Their right in money is the test of their right in property, and in their own labor. Their right in money involves all the important points of the conflict between freedom and slavery, with greater ease and less responsibility resting on the money-lender, than rested on the slave-master.

CHAPTER II.

***

WHY LENDING MONEY FOR INTEREST IS WRONG.

It may be seen from common reason that no person has a right to take from another more than he gives, unless he accepts it as a gift of friendship, or acknowledges it as a gift of charity. If he takes increase, that is, more than he gives, in any other way, it is clear that he is an oppressor, a thief, or a robber. The nature of the crime is determined by the circumstances connected with the taking. If the need of others is taken advantage of as a means to extort increase, it is oppression, or robbery, depending upon the circumstances of the case. If the increase is taken through deception it is theft. By whatever means taking from others more than is given is effected, unless it is accepted as a gift of friendship or a charity, it is an offense against justice and right. The custom of society and the law uniting to make money a necessity to the people in their worldly affairs, while they are prevented by the same authority from producing it, presents an opportunity that is never or rarely offered to the holders of any other thing, for the holders of money to take from others more than they give. The act of holding money to lend for interest, is an offense against the rights of all the people in money ; while taking more in other matters than is given, very rarely, if it ever, effects any but those from whom it is taken. Taking usury or increase on what is given in other things, marks the individual as an oppressor, and people will avoid him ; for they are not compelled to deal with him, as they are with one who stops the money from circulating in exchange for labor and property. The wrong will not only be limited in extent, but the perpetrator will be punished by neglect and loss of business, and will be checked in the evil practice. Taking increase on any other thing cannot be compared with lending money for

interest, nor can either of them be compared
to making gain in business

GAIN IN BUSINESS

is no evidence that increase is taken, or that
more is taken than is given. To illustrate the
proposition, we will take the example of a
merchant, who prepares a storehouse and fills
it with goods, to sell to his neighbors. If he
faithfully consults the good of his customers,
he can scarcely avoid giving them more than
they give him in profits ; as they would learn
by experience, if they were forced to get
along without the office, or function of the
merchant, being filled for them. If he takes
more from them in profits than he gives them
in goods and in the services that he renders
them, they will soon quit his store. It would
be a rare situation in business, where people
would be compelled to deal with a merchant
who took more in profits than an equivalent
for his recurring outlay, and for the goods
and services that he gave to his customers.
What is true of a merchant in this respect, is
true of every other honest and faithful person

in business. If they are true and faithful, they give more than they take. If they purposely take more than they give, they, too, are usurers. To give a clear example of a business person giving more than he takes, let the intelligent and careful publisher of a newspaper be instanced. Consider the important fund of useful information that is given in a carefully prepared weekly newspaper, for three or four cents per week, and it will be seen that it is quite possible for business people to give more than they receive, and still make gain. The money-lenders alone, from the nature of their business, must be chargeable with taking more than they give, and they stand condemned by the Word of God, and by the sore experience of untold millions, as the oppressors of their kind. That the borrower frequently makes more than the interest upon the money borrowed, is no refutation of the charge that the money-lender takes more than he gives. It merely shows that the borrower has either unwittingly or purposely become a participant in oppressing the rest of the people. For the interest or

2

increase is not in the money borrowed, nor in
the services of the lender ; and if it is taken,
it must be taken from other people. Increase
means more than, or above the thing increased ; and when a person takes back all that he
gave, and something more than or above what
he gave, the circumstances of the case determine whether he is a recipient of a gift of
friendship or of charity, or whether he is a
usurer. To give in friendship is often the
only way the giver can do the good that he
wants to do ; but there is no doubt that the
giver, when he bestows the gift upon a worthy
person, reaps the highest reward of the two
in satisfaction. True people in business try
to give more than they receive, and are blessed
with a blessing that the takers of increase
cannot receive, or comprehend. While these
truths may be seen through common reason,
we quote the sure foundation for them from the
Word of God : " Take thou no usury of him
or increase ; but fear thy God, that thy brother
may live with thee. Thou shalt not give him
thy money upon usury, nor lend him thy vic-
tuals for increase."—LIVITICUS, xxv, 36, 37.

CHAPTER III.

CIRCULATION OF MONEY.

The circulation of money is often spoken of, and people pass along the remarks that are made on the subject in conversation, without noticing what the words do, or what they ought to, import. For instance, it is customary to hear the act of borrowing money to pay a debt, or taxes, or to buy produce, or other things as circulating money ; without considering that the larger part of the operation consists in taking the money back to the lender, with the required additions in the form of interest ; although there may be, and generally is, but a few days between the different parts of the transaction. And without considering the fact that the interest paid, together with the evident immunity from competition in business that the money-lender enjoys, may at the time be causing people to take money out of business, to be used in lending for interest, instead of continuing to circulate it in business. Now, suppose that the average time of loans of money to business people is sixty days, it is evident that after the money is once out, instead of circulating, the operation is a constant contraction of circulation. The business has been in operation long enough now, to afford a view of the other side. Let us go into the counting-rooms of the borrowers, and see what is going on there. Look at that careful man bending to the inspection of his business, to see where he may hope to draw out money, for the sixty days are passed, and he has only the days of grace left. After long hesitation, and with deep concern mingled with pain, he now makes drafts upon customers, that he knows ought not to be drawn. He is conscious that in precipitating these drafts upon these careful business men, his customers, it will inevitably disturb the business relations; but it must be done; the money must be returned to the lender, with the interest. The

drafts are made and sent. We will now take
a look into the counting-rooms of the men to
whom the drafts have just been presented.
They go now to the work of examining accounts; they find their business standing fair,
but working close. There appears to be no
margin of money. They accept and pay the
drafts; but take a hint, also, that business is
working too close; and they determine to
contract the borders of their operations.
These contractions effect others, and vibrate
through business, till every branch is touched
by them. So business goes on ; the borrowing continues up to its old volume, but each
evening the circulation is less by the sum of
the interest of that day, than it was in the
morning. The people are now conscious that
money is becoming very scarce in their affairs,
and they become more careful in parting with
it. The motions of money become much
slower in consequence, and the same amount
of money does much less business ; while the
amount in business is actually becoming less
day by day, and its motions continue to get
slower in a corresponding ratio. Any person

can recognize the picture as the true likeness of the existing condition of the country ; and they can also see at a glance that the picture, like the condition, gives no hope of anything better, so long as business runs in existing channels. They can certainly see, also, that borrowing money on promises to return it to the lender with increase, does not circulate money, but the reverse ; and that the only way to circulate money is to give it out in exchange for labor and property. *The more and oftener that money is borrowed and returned to the lenders with interest, the faster it contracts the circulation ; and in an equal degree practically changes the purpose of money, from that of supporting the business of the government, and all the people, to that of supporting the money-lenders*

CHAPTER IV

STANDARD OF VALUE AND MEDIUM OF EXCHANGE.

In a work entitled "Money and the Mechanism of Exchange," by W. Stanley Jevons, M. A., F. R. S., Professor of Logic and Political Economy in the Owens College, Manchester, and published by D. Appleton & Co., 549 and 551 Broadway, New York, there is much information given on subjects connected with merchandising in money. Also, a broad, rickety foundation for the business of lending money for interest. We quote here from the book, that part which appears to be offered as a foundation for money-lending, with the explanatory connections, as found in the first and second sections of the third chapter.

"We have seen that three inconveniences attach to the practice of simple barter; namely, the improbability of coincidence between persons wanting and persons possessing; the complexity of exchanges, which are not made in terms of one single substance; and the need of some means of dividing and distributing valuable articles. Money remedies these inconveniences, and thereby performs two distinct functions of high importance, acting as

(1) A medium of exchange.

(2) A common measure of value.

In its first form money is simply any commodity esteemed by all persons, any article of food, clothing, or ornament which any person will readily receive, and which, therefore, every person desires to have by him in greater or less quantities, in order that he may have the means of procuring the necessaries of life at any time. Although many commodities may be capable of performing this function of a medium, more or less perfectly, some one article will usually be selected, as money *par excellence*, by custom or the force of circumstances. This article will then begin to be used as a measure of value. Being accustomed to exchange things frequently for sums of money, people learn the value of other articles in terms of money, so that all exchanges will most readily be calculated and adjusted by comparison of the money values of the things exchanged."

By the foregoing the public need of money as a measure of value, and medium of exchanging value, is well shown. The author appears to have a peculiar taste in this instance for putting his horse to the hind end of the cart, and making money a medium of exchanging value, before people have learned its use as a measure of value. He says that after money has been adopted, " by custom or force of circumstances, as a medium of exchanging value, this article will then begin to be used as a measure of value." And he adds, " being accustomed to exchange things frequently for sums of money, people learn the value of other articles in terms of money, so that all exchanges will most readily be calculated and adjusted, by comparison of the money values of the things exchanged."

It would appear from the last sentence that the author did not like the look of things while the horse was at the wrong end of the cart, and people were exchanging values in money, before they had learned its use as a measure of value, and he concluded to take the horse away altogether.

Now it appears to be his meaning that the people use money as a medium of exchanging value, before they learn the value of it; but being selected, by the use of it, as a medium of exchanging value, this article will then begin to be used as a measure of value.

Having learned the value of things by the money measure, people cease to use money as a medium of exchanging value, and most readily adjust all exchanges by comparison of the money values of the things exchanged.

That looks like an improvement. The horse had better be away. But now he puts the horse back again, and again to the hind end of the cart; for he says: " A third function of money soon develops itself. Commerce cannot advance far, before people begin to borrow and lend, and debts of various origin are contracted. It is in some cases usual, indeed, to restore the very same article which was borrowed, and in almost every case it

would be possible to pay back in the same
kind of commodity.   If corn be borrowed,
corn might be paid back, with interest, in corn ;
but the lender will often not wish to have
things returned to him at an uncertain time,
when he does not much need them, or when
their value is unreasonably low.   A borrower,
too, may need several different kinds of articles, which he is not likely to obtain from one
person, hence arises the convenience of borrowing and lending in one generally recogniz-
ed commodity, of which the value varies little.
Every person making a contract by which he
will receive something at a future day, will
prefer to secure the receipt of a commodity
likely to be as valuable then as now.   This
commodity will usually be the current money,
and it will thus come to perform the function
of a *standard of value.*   We must not suppose
that the substance serving as a standard of
value is really invariable in value, but merely
that it is chosen as that measure by which the
value of future payments is to be regulated.
Bearing in mind that value is only the ratio
of quantities exchanged, it is certain that no

substance permanently bears exactly the same value relatively to another commodity ; but it will, of course, be desirable to select as the standard of value, that which appears likely to continue to exchange for many other commodities in nearly unchanged ratios."

From the position the professor gained under the head of a medium of exchange and a common measure of value established by custom, or the force of circumstances, he finds people will begin to borrow and lend, and that " every person making a contract by which he will receive something at a future time, will prefer to secure the receipt of a commodity likely to be as valuable then as now. This commodity will usually be the current money, and it will thus come to perform the function of a standard of value."

A measure of value, when it is adopted by sufficient authority, becomes a standard of value. He had the measure of value established by the strongest known authority, that is, by custom or the force of circumstances ; but he does not find it to be a standard of value till people begin to lend it to be paid back in kind. When money is loaned, to be paid back in kind, the act values money at a future time, as compared with itself at the present time. A value set for a future time, of course, would be in the nature of a guess, but as there is in lending money always an advance in the value of money over its value at the present time, and as an advance in the value of money makes a decline in the things that money measures the value of, it must be admitted that there is great propriety in the guesses, for they make their own fulfillment sure. The Professor might, with great propriety, have said that thus it came to perform the function of a measure of value; a dishonest measure, always expanding to take unjust gains. But he could with no propriety say that thus it performs the functions of a standard of value; for those who use it always change values by it. He will hardly claim that it is the function of a standard to make changes against others, at the will and for the gain of the interested parties who use it.

Falsity is the garb of evil, and a writer describing and tolerating an evil, will be sure to clothe it in falsity, if he makes his language consistent with his work. Professor Jevons was writing a book on money. In the work he came to the point at which evil desires prompt men to take advantage of others, by taking money out of its function in business, and holding it to lend for interest, an evil that in its every act injures the public rights in money. If he had had any (the least) of the reformer in the constitution of his mind, he would have seen the evil. But he is no reformer; he appears to be entirely satisfied, and if advance is to be made, he will look for it in the straight line of existing conditions. He saw no evil in money-lending. But he was compelled to recognize and account for it in his work; he did this, and he gave it the most comely dress that it was capable of wearing. It is the greatest evil extant in worldly affairs; and he clothed and surrounded it with falsity and rags. The only thing remarkable is that he should be so entirely unconscious of what he was doing.

We will now look over the ground for ourselves. We will suppose that in the early

stages of the question of selecting and adopt-
ing money, two men meet in business ; one of
them has gold, and the other has corn ; and
they want to make an exchange of a part of
their commodities. They will not exchange
by even weights, or even bulks. It is evident
that they must fix a value for one of the commodities by bulk or by weight, and then ascer-
tain the quantity of the other that will agree
with the value fixed for that one. They
know that corn can be increased indefinitely,
and that it is very perishable ; it will not,
therefore, be suitable for a measure of value.
But gold is limited in supply, and is very
little subject to change ; and for these reasons
it is very suitable for a measure of value.

They value gold by weight, therefore, and
then determine what the corn is worth by
the gold measure. That being done they are
ready to make the exchange, using the fixed
value of gold as the measure of value, and
gold itself at its fixed value as the medium of
exchange. They have now erected gold into
a measure of value and a medium of exchange,
and they show the convenience of it to others ;

and they adopt it also. When it has become customary to value things by the gold measure and exchange values in gold, they go to government, and it adopts it, and by law makes it the only legal sign of value, and legal tender.

Thus it becomes a standard of value, and a standard medium of exchange.

By custom and by law all are now compelled to procure money to pay business balances and taxes, or they can hold no property or do no business. Certain sharp ones now see the *grand opportunity* and they exchange their property for money, and refuse thereafter to do business that will require paying out the money. Soon the need of the money that they extracted from business channels presses heavily upon other people, and they go to the holders of the money, not to borrow it, for they know that those who " go borrowing go sorrowing ;" but they go to exchange services or property for the money.

Oh, no ! the holders of the money do not want labor or property ; but they will lend it on condition that it will be paid back to them with more money. And now, in the palliating, not to say deceptive, words of Prof. Jevons, " Commerce cannot advance far before people begin to borrow and lend, and debts of various origin are contracted." The statement of the condition carries positive proof on its face, that the people cannot perform the tasks that the money-lenders force upon them by taking the money out of business and holding it to lend.   In the nature of things, money-lending, if it is allowed to become general, will subject all business and labor to itself. Many things may exist that may help to hold a sort of depressed life in business. As, for instance, large collections of taxes and revenues, to be disbursed among the people, in pensions, annuities and salaries. While this governmental control of large sums of money may make it possible for business among the people to retain some vitality, it is a slavish life for the masses of the people, and they cannot help but sink deeper and deeper into poverty and degradation.

There is a view of the effects of the control of the money of the country as interest-bear-

ing capital, that all are interested in keeping
before them, and especially the laboring and
producing millions.   That is, that an interest
or inducement that acts to restrain the exchange of money for labor or property, the
product of labor, is borne and paid by those
who labor and produce property ; and it is
paid on every dollar's worth of business that
springs from and is connected with labor and
property.   If the interest is one per cent. the
producers pay it on all the business operations
that are measured by money, and not merely
on the actual money borrowed in transacting
the business ; and they pay as much additional
as the condition produces restraint upon the
exchange of money for labor and property.
Thus the one per cent. to-day reduces the
prices of the product of labor by that amount.
But after the reduction is established the one
per cent. acts with as much force for another
reduction of one per cent.

This goes on, step after step, and in time
creates such distrust of values of labor and
property, that money will not be exchanged
for them on any reasonable or measurable

terms. From these plain principles it can be seen how utterly the present rates of interest are grinding the producers, and how foolish or wicked those politicians are who want the government to issue money that would be interchangeable at the will of the holders into United States bonds, bearing interest at the rate of three and sixty-five one-hundredths per cent. These politicians would not add straws to the already over-loaded camel's back, but mill-stones.

CHAPTER V.

PROPERTY RENT AND INTEREST.

It is not necessary to draw a parallel between rent of property and interest on money for those who will give the subject a little thought, but as there are some who do not take the trouble to examine it, but blindly defend money-lending, we will illustrate the difference by an example of a man who rents a farm.

When a man rents a farm, he pays for what he receives of the store laid up in the farm, and which he does not return. The amount he pays is not determined by the money invested in the farm. In other words, the rent is not calculated on what the farm cost the owner in money, but is fixed by the productiveness of farms of its kind. If the owner asks more than the other party can reasonably

draw out of the farm, he will not take it.
Farms are property made by the people.
They are neither limited as money is, nor are
the people compelled to take those already
improved, but may improve others until the
supply brings the demands for rent to reasonable terms.   Money, on the other hand, is not
made by the people, but is a creation of society and law, and the law compels all to use it,
or own no property and do no business.   It
can only be gotten by the people in exchange
for labor or property; but when the holders
refuse to part with it for labor or property,
people are compelled to borrow it.   When
they have paid it back, they have returned all
they received, and if they pay interest they
return more than they received, which is usury,
and is forbidden by the Word of God.   As it
is prohibited by the Word of God, it might
be concluded at once, from that alone, that it
is violative of the principles of justice among
men.   If a person takes more rent for a farm
than would represent the portion that reasonably would be taken from the store laid up
therein, he also would be taking usury; he

would be taking without giving, and would be a usurer. But society and government would not be participants with him in the evil, as they had not prevented the renter from making a farm for himself, and had not made the farm an unavoidable necessity to him. Society and government prevent people from making money, and, at the same time, place a necessity upon all the people to procure and use it. Thus they become participants in oppressing individual members of society, if they allow people to make gain by charging interest for the use of money. The difference between taking interest for money and making gain by handling property, may be illustrated further by people taking rent for houses. A house for people to live in represents a store of uses and service performed for those who live in the house. The store consists of many things, namely, the building and grounds, the main parts of which it is supposed, the renter returns when he leaves the house; and the wear and tear of the house from time and usage; the time and expense of the owner, in looking after the property, and keeping it in repair ; and taxes and insurance.   All of the items but the main portions of the house and grounds are used by the renter and kept, and the rent that he pays is for what he keeps, and not for the things he returns,   There may be as much disposition in the owner of a house to take increase on the things returned, as there is to make gain by taking interest on money, but the opportunity is rarely afforded ; and when it is done, it effects none but the individuals concerned in the transaction.   If the holders of money are allowed to make gain by charging interest for the use of it, they will cease to part with it for services and property ; and will, as they are doing now, subject all people to themselves, and take the labor and property for the use of the money, and while they degrade all others to vassalage, they will own both the money and property.   It is therefore the duty of society and government to follow up with confiscation, all acts of taking interest or increase on private promises to pay money ; for it is the sum of all oppressions among men, and it is made possible, and edge is given to it, by the laws

of government. That is, by government
making money of limited material, or limiting
the amount that may be made ; and making it
the only legal sign of value, and legal tender.

As farms are made of parts of the earth's
surface, by authority of the laws of government, while "the earth is the Lord's," and made
for all his children, it is doubtless right for
society and government to be careful how the
earth's surface is apportioned out. The movement against granting large tracts of it to
corporations is in the right direction, but
there might be further advance made in the
same direction with propriety, and in time
doubtless must be. But under the diversified
order of productive employments existing in
civilized society, it may be a long time before
a farm or a piece of the earth's surface to cul-
tivate, will become an imperative necessity to
any individual. Whereas the law makes
money an imperative necessity to all of the
people, therefore, the protection of the right
that every individual has in money, is the
present need of society, and is the most imperative duty that government could perform.

CHAPTER VI.

TIME OF MONEY.

It is seen in business affairs that there are stoppages in the circulation of money from various causes. It is claimed that if the money is deposited in bank, that the banker can safely lend it into the active business affairs of the country, in quantities agreeing with the average stoppage of the money.

The stoppage of money in business while the sums to be moved are being collected, and other circumstances attendant on its movements are being prepared, is wholesome; and it works no inconvenience but what has a very good effect in business affairs. Depositing the money for safe keeping, if the owner thinks it best to do so, would be orderly; but it cannot be loaned by the banker without introducing many disorders. First, it offers an easy way of supplying what, at the time, might be only a temporary deficiency of money in the business of the borrower; and turns the attention from the necessity of taking up the dropped stitch that caused the deficiency, and hurries the business to the fatal " nine deficiencies." Second, it incites to efforts to climb into fortunes through speculations, rather than through the slow, regular steps of productive industry. Turning money more and more out of regular productive business, inflicts continually increasing difficulties upon those engaged in such business; and gives a general horror of regular business as the fountain of trouble. Finally, over the wild waste that money-lending works in productive business, it is made manifest to all that money is the one commanding and desirable thing of the world ; and the effort to get money out of business and property, becomes the ruling motive among men. Everything useful is lost sight of in the effort to abstain from employing money; and saving money is the one essential business of life. Lending money for gain is a wrong inflicted upon society; and

saving the time of money is only a false
thought to excuse the wrong. It has been
said that lending money turns the money from
productive business. This results from the
things adduced, and also from the fact that all
of the movements of money require time to
prepare for them; consequently there is a
large consumption of the time of money in
preparing return movements to the money-
lenders. This movement is in a direction
from business, and unlike a movement in the
direction of business, it projects no life, but
the reverse, through business channels, while
the money is being collected. When the
movement back to the lender is effected, the
money is out of business to remain so, until a
borrower takes it and starts it on a new course.
But this, when it takes place, leaves all of the
breaks that were made in business connections
by collecting the money out of business to
return it to the lender. The waste of the
time of money in preparing and making the
return movement to the lenders, and the increase of money that it takes out of circulation as interest above what it puts into circu-

lation, together with the breaks that such
movements make and leave in established
business relations, all disturb and discourage
productive business, and cause money to be
taken out of such business.   The time of
money belongs to the business in which it is
engaged, including the time required to collect the sums, and the necessary stoppage
while its movements are being prepared.   If,
in the meantime, the money is put into any
other business, events prove, that the money
ceases to belong to the first business, and that
it does belong to the last.   If the last business is banking and money-lending, the money
belongs to that business, and does not, and
cannot, belong to productive business.   The
merchant, when he takes his money to a banker to be loaned, lays the foundation for a business that will surely overthrow all regular productive employments.   Every business has a
right to direct the movements of the money
that is engaged in it.   If lending money for
gain is right, then the money must obey the
will of the lenders, and must seek such employment as can be hurried through its move-

ments. This, we know, takes place when bankers lend the money that is deposited with them. The money leaves the slow-moving, productive employments, and seeks such speculations as may be consistent with frequent returns of the money to the lenders.

The necessities of the people will induce them to try to do business, and through increasing troubles they will borrow money for business and to pay taxes. But day by day they feel more acutely how abject and galling the yoke is, that the practice of money-lending places upon productive employments.

CHAPTER VII.

CAPITAL AND LABOR.

A solution of the purpose and true use of money, will settle the question between capital and labor. This question has puzzled political economists for ages; and the more that has been said or written upon the subject, the further from solution it appears to be. Without stopping to consider the shades of meaning in the term capital, that appear to be the sources of confusion, as to the relation that exists properly between capital and labor, I will define the word by a feature of its meaning, by which all will recognize it; that is, accumulation. The man has accumulation of powers of body and mind greater than the boy, and in this he has more capital than the boy. The man uses his powers in performing the various functions that devolve upon him as a man, and he acquires more power and skill of body and mind, and also rewards of his usefulness in worldly things. Now he has more capital and of different kinds. It is very evident that in such accumulation or capital, there can be no possible conflict with any person else in the whole universe, unless the accumulations are used in a wrong direction, and for a wrong purpose. If accumulations are used in a direction that comes in conflict with other men's rights, it is the best evidence in the world of a wrong use of capital ; and society must not clip and form other men's interest to the capital, but must teach the true direction and use of capital, and clip the capital when it runs in a wrong direction. In the worldly affairs of men, it is necessary to have money, as a means of representing and exchanging values in a condensed and easily-handled form, and as a medium of contributing support to the government. To fit the money for the purpose, it must be made under authority of government; must be in limited, and as nearly as possible, in uniform supply ; and there must exist between human

services and property (the things to be valued),
and money, an interchangeable relation. These
necessary qualities of money are secured by
making it of gold and silver, or limiting it to
a gold and silver basis, and by making it the
only legal sign of value and legal-tender in
payment of private and public dues. The
character and function of money require its
circulation in all business affairs, and also that
the people shall procure it to pay their business balances and taxes. As the people are
not allowed to produce money, it is evident
they must get it of others, in business. At
this point there is a possibility that those who
have accumulations, that is, capital, will use it
in a way that will inflict great injustice upon
all other people. Money being necessary to
all, and existing in limited supply, by turning
their accumulations of property into money,
they have in their hands the means of controlling the labor and property of all other
people. If they now refuse to let the money
circulate in exchange for labor and property,
they raise a conflict in the business affairs of
the world. Their accumulation of knowledge

and skill may find exercise in blinding the
people as to where the evil lies, and to point
out relations between capital and labor, that
will harmonize with their handling of their
accumulations. The plain and easy mode of
harmony was by enslaving labor, but this has
a harsh sound in the present age; and now
they try it through what they call the rights
of capital. They falsely apply the truth that
there should be no conflict between capital
and labor, to the evil handling they make of
their accumulations; though they are making
the system of business among men unsound
and corrupt from head to foot; the head pam-
pered vice, and the body squalor and corrupt-
ing servility; yet they get the sanction of
statesmen and learned writers on political
economy, or, at least, are not rebuked by them.
The condition of society, that is resulting
from the evil handling of capital in banking
and money-lending in civilized countries, is
well described by Cardinal Manning, in a re-
cent sermon, in which he refers to pauperism
in England. He says: "England, the rich-
est of all countries, has upon it a stain and a

4

shame, not to be found in countries which Englishmen assume to despise; he meant pauperism, an intensely demoralized state of society. Poverty in itself was an honorable state; but pauperism was something altogether distinct from poverty. Pauperism was that wrecked condition of men and of families, out of which there was no rising by any effort of their own. And what did it come from? It would take too long to endeavor to say. One reason he would state: the closeness of the hands and hearts, and the ignorance in which the rich lived and died, of the state of the poor, who lived and died round about their dwellings. The possession of wealth and prosperity generated a selfishness and uncon- sciousness of the sufferings of others, so that men were wrapped up in their own daily indul- gence, and were forgetful of those who were in want."

Cardinal Manning describes a condition that cannot fail to grow out of the manner in which the few are controlling the money in banking and money-lending. Its direct and inevitable effect is to produce a state of wrecked, demoralized pauperism, that the mass of the people cannot possibly avoid falling into, much less, being in it, can raise themselves out of it. He describes the condition of both rich and poor, and leaves it to be inferred that the rich ought to help the poor; but he leaves the cause of the condition untold, unless we are to understand that it is because the rich do not help the poor. If the Cardinal intended to lay the cause to the neglect of the rich to give material support to the poor, it would be in harmony with an error of the Catholic church. It has undoubtedly been an error of that church to collect largely from the people, and then give support to the indigent, without sufficiently considering whether much of the indigence was not induced by the too heavy collection. The right rule for church, state, or individual, is first of all to be sure that you do not " lay grievous burthens upon men's shoulders," and when you give, be very sure that what you give has not been obtained by wrong and oppression ; when all observe the rule of unoffending right, it will be found that people of sound body and mind, will prefer to support themselves, and the number of the receivers of alms will be wonderfully lessened. Then such a condition as the Cardinal describes, both as to the rich and poor, would necessarily be greatly reduced, both in volume and virulence.

Why the Cardinal did not point out particularly the cause of the condition that he described, cannot be known. The occasion could not fail to be as appropriate to explain the cause, as to refer to the condition. We know that the money-lenders, by forcing people to abstain from business, and from the use of property, unless they will borrow money of them, are bringing about, for the laboring and business classes, the condition that is described by the Cardinal. Money-lending cannot fail to force the producing classes continually deeper and deeper into want and degradation. The business literally takes people by the throat, and says to them, " serve me."

CHAPTER VIII.

FINANCE.

The term finance, as connected with State affairs, and which, no doubt, is the connection that it was formerly most properly used in, signifies the money and revenues of the State. As connected with the science of political economy, it includes the proper mode of rais-ing and handling the State money or reven-ues. The term, as it is applied in the United States, signifies money in general, or in gov-ernmental affairs, and also in individual affairs. There appears to be nothing in the term itself that would vary its signification when applied to individual affairs, from what it would be when applied to State affairs. In the partic-ular as well as general application, it means the settlement, payment, or end ; or it means money, the thing by which the end is reached, and settlement and payment made. The gov-

ernment ordains that money shall be the settlement of, or payment of, or end of, all civil
affairs; hence money means finance or end,
and finance means money or end, whether in
private or in State affairs; and the getting of
money means the way to the end. Again, as
getting money is the way to end things in
money, getting money is included in the term
finance. The term finance, then, means the
art and science of getting money, and paying
or ending business affairs in money.

Finance is the result of production and
trade, and the science of production and trade
is the science of finance. As finance means
money, and includes getting money, and settlement and payment in civil affairs, while all
these result from production and trade, it is
clear that finance results from production and
trade; hence the science of production and
trade is the science of finance, and consequently that the mysteries of production and
trade, are the much talked-of

MYSTERIES OF FINANCE;

no more and no less. It must be borne in
mind that money is a sign or representative

of value, adopted by society and legalized by government, to settle and finish civil affairs. It is readily seen that the things to be settled, ended, or finished, grow out of doing, owning and trade. That is, out of production and trade. Without production and trade, there would be no civil affairs to be settled, and consequently there would be no need of money, and no such thing as finance. Finance, then, rest upon production and trade, begins where they begin, and stops where they stop. Now we see that the mysteries of finance are the merest myth, unless we understand by the mysteries of finance, the mysteries of production and trade. An individual to conduct successfully the affairs of a vegetable garden to supply a city market with wholesome and pleasant vegetables in their season, must master the mysteries of production and trade, in one of its most varied and intricate forms, with all of its parts very highly organized and in active operation to vary results. Yet common men do master the mysteries of this intricate specimen of the art and science of production and trade, and its resulting finance, with high success and pleasure ; unless their business is blighted by unusual agencies over which they have no control.

A merchant trading in foreign countries masters the mysteries of production and trade and resulting finance, though very many active forces conspire to make or modify the field to be occupied, and operated upon.   If these men master the mysteries of production and trade and resulting finance, what is the matter with statesmen, that they stand back with such awe before the word finance, which merely expresses the resultant effect of the active forces that others understand and harmonize ? What is there in the word ? A mere name.

To understand this mysterious awe of statesmen and politicians before the term money or finance, we must look further and more closely into the subject. We have seen that a common man will successfully carry on a vegetable garden, and reach the end, finance, or money, that he had to keep in mind and work towards in the whole business ; though the operation is a very complex one, and active

forces of both physics and metaphysics operate upon all parts of his business to modify
results.   The man knows this fact in its general action upon his business, and that he
must bring his operations to harmonize in a
great degree, with these active forces.   If he
fails in any particular, he will know why he
fails, and will modify or change that particular
part; but will go on, and in the main succeed,
unless, as said before, some unusual agency
changes the conditions.   If he fails in consequence of such unusual occurrence, the origin
and nature of the occurrence may be a mystery to him.   But if he fails without such unusual cause of failure, he will understand why
he failed, and can point out the cause, unless
he is lacking the degree of intelligence that
was required in his business.

What then, we ask again, is the matter with
the statesmen and politicians, that they should
stand awe-struck before what they call the
mysteries of money or finance?   They know
what money is, why money is, how it is made,
and what it is for.   Knowing all of these
things, and every one of them, with the exact-

ness that belongs to written law, they ought to
be able to point with unerring certainty to any
wrong that might occur in connection with
money or finance. Of all things that effect
the interest of men, money has the least mystery about it. It is adopted to simplify the
affairs of the people and government, and *do
away with mystery*. If money performs its
function, it removes mystery from all business
relations. If it does not perform its function,
why does it not ? Being a creature of society
and government, its purpose and function
ought to be well understood and defined, and
when it fails, or results in evil, a remedy ought
to be plainly and easily seen. As a starting-
point in investigating financial matters, it must
be constantly borne in mind that society and
government not only introduce a convenience
into the business of society and government,
by making money and organizing in it the
control of labor and property, but they do a
great deal more. They lay a necessity upon
every member of society to constantly procure and use money in their worldly affairs.
This affords an opportunity for the holders of

money to retire it from business, and hold it to lend for interest; and in that way take under their influence the entire business, property, and labor of the people, as their servants and for their gain.

This they have done, and the evil is making society quake to the center, the world over; while statesmen, with less wisdom than the cultivators of a vegetable garden, are awe-struck, and say "they do not understand the mysteries of finance."

CHAPTER IX.

INTERCHANGEABLE GREENBACK CURRENCY.

The movement in favor of issuing a currency, interchangeable at the will of the holder, into United States interest-bearing bonds, doubtless finds support from a few persons who are honestly seeking a way to stop the business of the people on its course to utter destruction; but that it originated with any who were making an honest effort to alleviate the sufferings of the masses, and to perform for their fellow-beings and country an unselfish service, it is not possible to believe, when we consider what the effect of such a system of currency would be. Ever since the money in common use in business, was elevated from the condition of what was known in 1836 and 1837 as "wild-cat money," there has been a continually increasing practice of taking money out of business and property, and holding it to lend for interest.

This practice had progressed so far as to cause, in 1857, what is known as the panic of that year in business. The stringency continued to increase at that time, but the war of the rebellion breaking out in 1861, the government was compelled to make and issue to the people, large sums of money in exchange for property and services. The money so issued sustained business while it lasted, notwithstanding the exhausting process of banking and money-lending. But when the war issues were over and exhausted, business began to reel and stagger, and is now prostrate ; while the money lies in the banks, and the process of transferring the property from the debtor to the creditor, as the producing and money-lending classes are respectively called, goes on. The prostrate condition of business is the result of capturing the money, and holding it to lend. People sell property, and get money in exchange for it. They now refuse to let it continue to circulate in exchange for labor and property, but part with it thereafter only on promises for its return to them with additional money. This places the productive classes under the necessity to borrow the money to supply the channels of business, including the necessary stoppage of the money in the pockets of the people and in the public treasuries, while its movements are being prepared, and also return it with additional money to the lenders, at times set to suit their gain. If the conditions that are made for the producing classes by the business of banking and money-lending, and the requirements of bankers and money-lenders for their own safety and profit are borne in mind, we will be able to appreciate what the effect of issuing a currency interchangeable at the will of the holders, into United States interest-bearing bonds, would be, both upon the money-lending and producing classes. But to appreciate the full effect of such a measure, we must also bear in mind that the custom of society and the law of government, make money a constant necessity in business, as a medium of exchanging values and paying taxes ; and, as the people are not allowed to make money, they must exchange services and property for it. Now, if the holders refuse to continue the circulation in that way, directly the business and producing classes suffer for the money; and not being able to get it in exchange for their products, they borrow it, and pay it back with increase. Day by day the process increases their difficulties, and piles up debt against their class, in favor of the banker and money-lenders. Business begins to fail, labor fails, poverty intensifies and spreads, and money accumulates in the banks. Politicians are now called upon, to solve the enigma of the times. This is the condition of affairs in the first centennial year of the nation's existence.

One hundred years ago the Fathers of the Republic were called upon to resist the unjust demands of government, even through war with one of the most powerful nations upon the earth. They proved themselves equal to the requirements of the occasion. Their descendants, the statesmen of the present day, are asked to solve the enigma of production and business suffering for money; while the money lies in banks, waiting safe interest-bearing promises to pay money. The question is a very simple one, and involves nothing more profound than to enquire for what use money is made, and whether it is performing its use. If money is merchandise, made for the benefit of the money-lenders, and which they may use to break up the productive industries of the people, and take their property from them, the solution would naturally be different from what it would be if it was made for a medium of transacting the business of the government and people ; while money-lending is a disease or parasite, growing upon the body politic. If the money is for the money-lenders, and the laws of the government, that make it necessary in business and to pay taxes, are merely means furnished them by the government 'to break up productive employments, and to take the property from the people, the hard money theories, by which the money may be reduced in volume, have, at least, some small degree of application to the purpose of money. But their application to the purpose is remote, weak, and indirect, as compared to the plan of making the money interchangeable at the will of the holder, into

United States interest-bearing bonds. Under this plan the money-holders would wipe out of existence, all the money that they could not use directly for their purpose, and would take the interest-bearing bonds of the government instead. It relieves the money-holders of all danger of cheap money, and at the same time gives them a large volume of government bonds on which to draw interest, and if occasion suits, to again recover the money. It obviates all indirections that might grow out of the hard-money plan, in subjecting business and labor to the money-lenders. But if money is made to facilitate the transaction of business among the people, and as a just means in the hands of the government, to draw its support from the labor and property of the people, while its legal character and its limited volume are means to the end, and money-lending is a disease to be cured; then are politicians failures on the money question, and the greenback politicians the worst of all. They are worse than failures; they are evil innovators. More will be said on this subject in another chapter.

5

CHAPTER X.

INFLATION.

According to a statement of the New York *World*, as accredited to it by the Wood County (Ohio) *Sentinel*, of the 11th of May, 1876, A. D. White, President of Cornell University, read a paper before the Union League Club, in New York city, entitled " Paper Currency Inflation in France—How it Began." It says: " The Club Theatre was filled with members, all of whom listened attentively to the strong, hard-money document, notwithstanding many of them were, or had previously been, paper-money men."

If the President made the statements reported, and made them the basis for conclusions in favor of hard money, as claimed for them in the report, it was a remarkable performance; for the statements separately, as reported, do not support the conclusions claimed for them. And when put together, they are insufficient to support conclusions in favor of hard money. "After reviewing briefly the events which occurred toward the end of 1789, which created the financial embarrassments in France, and led to a new issue of paper currency, the lecturer said : Within a few months after the first issue, another issue of $400,000,000 was made, making the total issue $800,000,000, but with a solemn pledge that the total amount put in circulation should not exceed $1,200,000,000. But very soon this pledge was violated, under the popular pressure, and $400,000,000 more were issued, but with a solemn promise that the circulation should never exceed $1,400,-000,000. This, too, was violated, and the issues went on in a rapidly increasing ratio. These issues gave a great stimulus, temporarily, to speculation, gambling, and stock-jobbing, throughout the country. There arose, and was rapidly developed, a great debtor class, partly of those who bought the national real estate, paying a small part down, and in-

tending to pay the remainder in small install-
ments ; partly from those speculators and
gamblers in values, who had bought for a rise
in nominal values.   Commerce and manufactures, though at first stimulated, were soon paralyzed, and finally almost universally destroyed.   The mercantile interest, which supposed
that it was aided by this inflation, since the
prices of goods on the shelves of the merchants were raised, soon found that it was in-
jured, no less than other interests, since the
merchants had to attach to their goods prices
not only to cover the increase in nominal
value, but the risks from fluctuation ; the
number of buyers diminished, and payments
grew less certain.   Inflation brought the
worst evils of all upon the masses of the
nation, upon the people of small fortunes, and
upon the working class.   The uncertainty in
values having paralyzed manufactures, vast
numbers of workmen throughout the nation
were thrown out of employ, so that after
prices were inflated 200 or 300 per cent., the
wages of labor remained the same as before
the inflation.   At the great centers, a reckless

gambling in values, which spread into the country at large arose, which led men to look on steady labor and moderate gains with contempt. The idea of thrift was obliterated among the French people, though they are naturally one of the most thrifty of nations. Corruption of public men followed. Mirabeau, Chabot, Fabre D'Eglantine, and others, who, two or three years before, risked their lives from patriotic motives, had now become so involved in the speculating mania and luxurious living, that Mirabeau received bribes from the Court, and others received bribes for their votes in the National Legislature. At last a franc in gold was worth 288 francs in paper. The measures of the Directory were then sketched together, with the issue of the " Territorial Mandats," which came to be as gold. These mandats were issued with every guarantee for their security, in the best of the national real estate, yet they depreciated to thirty and even to fifteen per cent. before they were issued from the press, and at last fell to five per cent. The collapse was then described, and the ruinous state in which France was

left. After this vast amount of paper money,
36,000,000,000 " assignats " and 2,400,000,000
" mandats," had been repudiated, coin began
to come in easily and naturally, and trade
having been put on a solid basis, prosperity
was gradually restored."

The professor says—" these issues gave a
great stimulus, temporarily, to speculation,
gambling and stock-jobbing, throughout the
country." The fact alone of largely increasing the volume of money, is no reason or ex-
planation for speculation, gambling, or stock-
jobbing. Nor has the volume of money,
whether it be large or small, any tendency in
itself to produce such results. If such things
exist, it is not from or owing to the volume of
money, nor is it owing to the material that
money may be made of. But it is owing to
the use that is made of money ; and the use
that is made of it depends upon the laws of
the government regulating the creation, and
use of money. It may be safely affirmed, as
the President of the University appears to
imply, that the handling of money in France
would be very much like the handling of

money in the United States, under the same or similar circumstances. To illustrate the fact that the volume of money, whether large or small, would not have in itself a tendency to beget " speculation, gambling, and stock-jobbing," we will suppose that the government of the United States, being in need of money, determines to print and issue four hundred million dollars of paper money. The government could not accomplish its purpose without a plan, and the plan would have to include the making, the issuing, and the circulation of the money. The circulation of a new issue of paper money, would spring from the fact that the government made it to be money, and thereby all private interests were formed into forces, to propel the circulation. If the government gave the new issue the legal character of money, and proper legislation prevented any private interest from springing up that would prevent the circulation, the money would, of necessity, enter into the function of measuring and exchanging values, in the business affairs of the government and people. The circulation of money is often a matter of necessity, even when the money is made of gold of the common standard. It circulates because the government and society make it the sign and representative of the value, that is in houses for people to live in, in clothes for them to wear, and in food for them to eat. It is altogether a regulation of society and government that an ounce of gold shall represent so many dollars' worth of the value of these things, or that gold shall represent value at all. The ordinance of the government propels the circulation by making it necessary in business, and to pay taxes and public revenues, when the money is of uncertain character. And when the value is of the fixed and stable character that belongs to the precious metals, the circulation is propelled by the desire and necessity to procure the services and property, the things of real value, that custom and law make the money the sign of. In a primitive state of society, it was not possible to establish confidence in the permanency in the value of money, and its interchangeability with property in any other way than by making it

of such metals as gold or silver. These metals
are but little subject to change or waste by
rust, and are limited in supply. These circumstances determined society and governments to make money of gold and silver, and
the choice of the metals for money, established the value of the metals. It is not the value
of the metals that give value to money, it is
the use that governments and society make of
money that gives it value. To secure an interchangeable relation between the representative value that society and government
give to money, and the real value that is in
labor and property, the government compels
the people to constantly use money in their
worldly affairs. This necessity induces the
people to exchange the real value they have
in their labor and property, for the representative value in money; notwithstanding that
the representative value cannot, in the nature
of things, be as true as the real value, even
when the money is made of gold or silver.
The government having by its laws, brought
the people to a willingness to exchange the
real value in their labor and property, for the

representative value in money, to the degree,
at least, of supplying themselves with money
to pay business balances and taxes and public
revenues ; there will be established an interchangeable relation between money, and labor
and property ; unless there proves to be a deficiency in the supply of money, or that the
holders of the money refuse to exchange it
for labor or property. If the exchange failed
because there was not sufficient money, it
would clearly be the duty of government to
lessen the taxes, or to increase the supply of
money. But if the exchange of labor and
property for money, to the degree of supplying
the necessary money for business, and to pay
taxes and public revenues, failed because the
holders of it would not exchange the fictitious
representative value in money, for the real
value that is in labor and property, it would
be conclusive proof that there was some wrong
at work, that was destroying all order among
men, and that it was determining the acts of
the holders of the money. For it cannot be
conceived that the holders of a fictitious representative would not exchange it for the real

thing represented, unless there was an extraneous inducement leading to the result. If the holders of the representative value in money were as willing to exchange it for the thing represented as the people will be to give the real for the representative, to the degree of supplying their business with necessary money and to pay taxes and revenues, the exchange will be made ; and business will go on among the people ; labor will be nourished, and production and consumption will both continually increase, and worldly prosperity will be attainable by all, as the reward of honesty and industry.   An increase in the volume, as long as the money would pay business balances and taxes, would not have a tendency to turn the money out of the real values that are in labor and property, but the reverse. When the holders of money retire it from business, by refusing to exchange it for labor and property, and by the process starve labor, a great wrong is inflicted upon the people, by means of the monetary laws of the government. And it is the duty of the learned to point out the wrong, and the cure for it.   And every

word of truth on the subject will satisfy reason.   But to say or imply that an increase in
the volume of money, or any other thing that
in its nature would lessen confidence in the
permanency of the representative value in it,
would cause the holders to refuse to exchange
it for the real values, is an absurdity on its
face.   Reason says at once, that if money re-
tires from productive business to deal in
shadows, it springs from another cause than
an increase of the volume of money.

What the cause was in France, may be inferred from the cause in the United States.
We know that the holders of money in our
country, retire it from business, and refuse to
exchange it for labor or property, because
they know the legal and social necessity there
is upon all the people to procure and use it
in connection with their worldly affairs; and
they retire it from business, and refuse to exchange it for labor or property, that they may
levy tribute upon the mass of the people, for
the use of it ; while by notes, and promises to
pay money, they still hold it under their own
control.   This handling of money, in its direct

effects, breaks up productive business; for common perception as well as experience tells the people that money cannot perform the functions that exist for it in business, and to pay taxes and public revenues, while it is held as private merchandise, and its value changed at will of the holders, for their own gain. And for their gain it is compelled to make periodical movements out of business to them.

The enterprising people seeing the impossibility of using money in the slow productive business, use it in speculation; and this runs into the gambling and stock-jobbing, described by the President of the University. The condition is in no degree owing to the volume of money, or on account of the material that it is made of; but is owing to the use that the owners of the money, that is, those who have it and do not owe it, make of it. If the government should over issue paper money, while it is all legal tender, and will pay taxes and public revenues, it will only make the people the more willing to turn it into property and labor, that produces property. And labor will only be the more sought after and encourag-

ed.   But when there is another use made of
money, namely, that of collecting tribute for
the use of it, the controllers of the money
break up all orderly business; for no amount
of money entering business, on promises to
make frequent return movements to the lenders, with additional money, can support business.   In such case, likewise, the money-holders have the greatest possible inducement to
have the volume of money reduced, as thereby all danger of competition among lenders
is removed, and their capital increased also.
That the holders of gold should make a great
difference between it and the paper-money,
would not check business, as long as the
paper would perform the function of exchanging values in business affairs, and pay taxes
and revenues of government.   This Professor
White might have seen in the United States
in 1864, when the difference between gold and
paper money was greatest; it had no tendency to check business.   The control of money
as a capital to lend, did even then check the
investment of the paper-money in real estate,
excepting in leading cities that were stimula-

ted at that time by the business of preparing army snpplies. As long as the people were able to get money that would pay taxes and business balances, as they were by the disbursements of the government for labor and property during the war, and until those disbursements were exhausted among the people, business went on and increased. But as soon as the disbursements fell from the war scale, and the money was exhausted among the people, and business had to depend on money that was borrowed on promises to return to the lender with increase, the death-struggles of business began, and go on to be ended only by the transfer of all property to the moneylenders, and subjugation of the laboring and productive classes to them.

There is no money in the United States now, nor has there been for the last thirty-five years, that the people were not willing and anxious to take in business, or in exchange for most valuable labor or property. Why is it that the money will not be exchanged for this labor or property? The refusal brought the business trouble of 1857, and is breaking up

all business now. If there is any meaning in
the statements attributed to Professor White,
it is that the money-holders refuse to put it
in business, or exchange it for labor or property, because it is inflated paper-money, and is
not gold, or reduced to a gold standard.

If the controllers of the money, and their
aiders and abettors, were not smitten by that
blindness that in all ages led those engaged in great public wrong to their utter overthrow, they would see the folly of their prac-
tices and teachings, and that they are standing over a volcano, with nothing but the thin-
nest possible crust under their feet. There is
no truth taught on the subject of taking interest on money, that the writer knows of, but
the neglected truth of the Word of God; and
it is not strange that there should be some
clamor for an increase of paper-money as the
Professor says there was in France. For in
the absence of true instruction, it would be
the remedy first thought of, for business fam-
ishing for money.

That there is so little of such clamor in the
United States, ought to admonish the money-

holders that they have a different order of mind to deal with. Mind that will suffer, and wait, and investigate, until the foundation principles of money are reached ; and being found, will build there, and will clear away everything that would obstruct the building, or mar the effect.

CHAPTER XI.

———

MONTESQUIEU ON MONEY-LENDING.

The business of lending money for interest has always been so influential among men, that it shaped or colored all learning and instruction on the subject of money and civil laws.

In the Divine Word alone is the truth retained on lending for interest, and the learned among men treat the *Divine Truth* on the subject as an antiquated and impractical idea or " counsel of religion."

Montesquieu, in his work entitled " Spirit of Laws," says :

" Specie is the sign of value.   It is evident he who has occasion for this sign, ought to pay for the use of it, as well as anything else he has occasion for.   All the difference is that other things may be either hired or bought ;

whilst money, which is the price of things, can only be hired and not bought."

Here, in a note, he says: "We speak not of gold and silver considered as merchandise." And continues: "To lend money without interest, is certainly an action laudable and extremely good; but it is obvious that it is a counsel of religion, and not of civil law. In order that trade may be successfully carried on, it is necessary that a price be fixed on the use of specie; but this should be very inconsiderable. If it be too high, the merchant who sees that it costs him more in interest than he can gain by commerce, will undertake nothing; if there is no consideration to be paid for the use of specie, nobody will lend it; and here, too, the merchant will undertake nothing. I am mistaken when I say nobody will lend; the affairs of society will ever make it necessary. Usury will be established, but with all the disorders with which it has been constantly attended. The laws of Mahomet confounded usury with lending upon interest. Usury increases in Mahometan countries, in proportion to the severity of the prohibition.

The lender indemnifies himself for the danger he undergoes of suffering the penalty. In those eastern countries, the greater part of the people are secure of nothing. There is hardly any proportion between the actual possession of a sum, and the hopes of receiving it again after having lent it. Usury, then, must be raised in proportion to the danger of insolvency.

" The greatness of maritime usury is founded on two things: the danger of the sea, which makes it proper that those who expose their specie, should not do it without considerable advantage; and the ease with which the borrower, by means of commerce, speedily accomplishes a variety of great affairs. But usury with respect to land-men not being founded on either of these two reasons, is either prohibited by the legislators, or what is more rational, reduced to proper bounds."

It is evident that if the members of society who have occasion to use money cannot buy it, that is, cannot get it in exchange for the things that it is the price of, but must hire the use of it, that is, must borrow it and pay it back with additional money, it will be impossible for society to exist. If money is borrowed and to be paid back with interest, the need of money to pay back the borrowed money will be greater by the sum of the interest, than the need of society. And if the affairs of society, as the author says, will ever make it needful, the paying back would come in the way of the succeeding needs of society, and would increase the succeeding needs by the whole weight of the previous needs, increased by the interest on the borrowed money; a condition that could not be borne, and society would be destroyed by its inability to get the necessary money.

The author is not speaking of the use of money in the affairs of society, that is merely for the convenience of society, and which might be supplied by the use of something else, or might be dispensed with; for, he says, he speaks not of gold and silver as articles of merchandise, but of money created by the law of the State. The need of money created by the law of the State, and by custom of society, is more than a mere convenience; and the

need will disorganize society, if it is not supplied. The author appears to have seen the
dilemma the condition placed society in, and
tried to excuse it by citing the failure of Mahometan laws to prohibit taking interest on
money. He then gives two reasons for high
interest on money to be engaged in maritime
affairs, but says " usury with respect to land-
men, not being founded on either of the reasons governing in the case of maritime usury,
is either prohibited by the legislators, or, what
is more rational, reduced to proper bounds."

If the principle he starts out with, that
those who have occasion to use money ought
to pay for the use of it, whilst they cannot
buy the money itself, is founded on reason
and the rights of the holders of the money,
it is hard to see by what authority the legislators would interfere to reduce the interest to
proper bounds, or to prohibit it, for the benefit of land-men, or any other people. Again,
if the failure of Mahomet to prevent interest
by severe legislation against it, is worth anything to prove that which he brought it up to
prove, that is, the impracticability of prevent-

RIGHTS OF THE PEOPLE IN MONEY.

RIGHTS OF THE PEOPLE IN MONEY.

ing interest by severe legislation against it, why does he suggest to legislators to prohibit it, or, as more rational, to reduce it to an inconsiderable quantity for the land-men?

It would naturally be as difficult to reduce interest to an inconsiderable quantity, as to prohibit it; for when it was so small as to be inconsiderable, there would be no, or but little, opposition to taking it off altogether; that is, to prohibit it. The learned author appears to have been dreadfully confused, by the question of interest on money. If he could have consented to let the light of the *Divine Truth* rest upon the question as it is in the Word of God, it would have enlightened his path so that he might have been able to travel in a consistent course. But when he started off with the intimation that that light was not sufficient to lead civil law, he might be expected to unsettle the foundation of his edifice as he did. He started out to excuse and justify lending money for interest. There is no foundation for reason in that direction, as his staggering shows. He was bold enough; at the first bound he vaulted into the position that money made by the government to be the sign of value, cannot be bought with the things that it is the sign of. He conveys the impression that the people have no right to expect money to circulate in that way, but must expect to borrow it, to be paid back with interest. From this irrational position, it could not be expected that he would advance rationally.

Besides the error that the writer of the "Spirit of Laws" makes, in taking it for granted that the holders of money have a right to lend it for interest, there are two other errors that are very generally committed, in considering the business of lending for interest. The first is, that the lenders of money are necessarily the main gainers in the operation; and the second error is that the legislation that may be instituted to correct the evil, ought to be directed to the protection of the borrowers, and for their benefit.

The business of lending money for interest is a public injury; and legislation to correct and prevent it, must be for the protection of the public, and the fines must inure to the government, the money-making power.

Montesquieu, in his " Spirit of Laws," quotes from Ulpian that " he pays least who pays latest," and says : " This decides the question whether interest be lawful ; that is, whether the creditor can sell time, and the debtor pay for it."

As a principle this is unsound, like all other things said in favor of the right to lend money for interest. The increased value of money at the time of the latest payment, may make it the greatest and best, without any increase in the quantity of the money. Gold dollars fluctuate in value very much, when they are tested by labor and property, the things that test the value of money. Any person who has been doing business in our country, in the years 1874 and 1875, knows that money, that is, gold, has appreciated nearly one hundred per cent. since that time, and is still very rapidly appreciating ; consequently a payment in gold now, would be fully twice as valuable as it would have been two years ago. The principle of the fluctuation of money as to value is shown by Professor Jevons, in his work entitled " Money and the Mechanism of Exchange."

In speaking of " *The Standard Unit of Value*," he says : " The expression *standard unit of value*, will indeed be almost certainly misunderstood as implying the existence of something of fixed value. As we have seen, however, (page 11) value merely expresses the essentially variable ratio in which two commodities exchange, so that there is no reason to suppose that any substance does for two days together, retain the same value. All that a standard of value means is, that some uniform, unchangeable substance is chosen, in terms of which all ratios of exchange may be expressed and calculated, without any regard whatever to the feelings or mental phenomena which the commodities produce in men. For reasons already stated, one of the metals, gold, silver, or copper, has usually been considered most suitable for constituting the standard substance."

Lending money for interest is a wrong against every human right in worldly business ; and when authors, even the most learned and wise on other things, try to excuse or justify it, they lose their wisdom and talk foolishly.

CHAPTER XII.

BANKING AND CLEARING-HOUSE SYSTEM.

To illustrate the result of business that is carried on under the now universal operation of money-lending and banking, we will look at the operation as it progresses every day around us. We see that nearly all the money that is received in business is immediately deposited in bank. By this operation all the money that can be said to be in business is brought out of the pockets of the people and all other places, and deposited once, at least, every ninety days. A great deal of it is deposited over and over again during that time. The disbursements in business are nearly all made by cheques and drafts against the deposits. These cheques and drafts rarely take up the money, but are entered to the credit of the persons to whom they are given ; and they carry as much of the deposits as they call for, to the credit of those persons. They again, by cheques or drafts, transfer the deposits to those persons to whom they want to make payments, who again have them entered on the books of the banks that they do business with, to their credit, and the money becomes their deposits in those banks, or pays debts, as the case may be. Of all the money that is deposited in bank, there is a very small portion taken up in money again, in the way of making disbursements in business. As said before, the bulk of all such disbursements are made by cheques or drafts against the deposits; and these cheques and drafts are balanced against each other, while the money to balance the account between the banks is sent to the banks that it is due to, by those that prove to be owing it. But of all the money that is gathered from the people by the operation of business, and which, as said before, in the course of about ninety days, takes all the money there is for business, there is but a small portion paid back to the people. On the contrary, from the day it enters the

banks it becomes capital in them to be held to
lend. And it never enters business again in
exchange for labor and property, the only
entry by which money can truly be said to be
in business. But when it leaves the banks it is
securely bound to return at a time set to suit
the interest of the banks, and to bring more
money with it; while the same money had
previously been borrowed of them on promises for its return with increase, and is now
owed many times over to them for itself.
Thus, once in ninety days, or less time, by the
operation of depositing the money in bank
and by the use of cheques and drafts, the
entire money used in business is swept into
the banks, to be added again to the debt of
the people, by their unavoidable borrowing of
the money, instead of getting it in their business, as they would if it was not for the
business of money-lending. But this, hard
as it is, is not all that the people have to
encounter from money-lending. There are
vast debts for borrowed money, controlled by
private money-lenders, and on these debts
there are large sums of money constantly

gathered and held for similar operations.
From these facts of the daily working of the
business of money-lending, it is seen that the
impossible task is laid upon the people to
borrow money and keep it in business and in
the treasuries of the country, and also at short
set times to return it all, many times increased,
to the banks and money-lenders; or, as the
alternative, to be ostracized from society. The
mere operation of withholding the money
from circulating in exchange for labor and
property, and compelling people to borrow it
on promise to return it with increase, in a very
few years after the operation was extended
over all the money, would break up business,
and transfer the property to the money-
lenders.   But this, with a general system of
depositing the money in banks, and disbursing by cheques and drafts in business, with
the operation of the clearing-house, would
enable the banks and money-lenders to absorb
a world every few years, if it would only be
put into their mill.   It is simply magnificent
on account of its proportions.

Lending money for interest must be extirpated by law, and hereafter prevented under penalty of confiscation of all money engaged in it to the government. Then business can be revived, and business people may unite for the purpose of clearing, if they choose. Professor Jevons claims that there is great advantage in it, by saving the use of money in a very large portion of business operations. The advantage may be reaped by the people, without cultivating the evil feature that the Professor appears to value so highly, namely, that of lending the money for interest. The selfish control of money breaks business. People should consider this fact from the effect that it has upon their own business, if they cannot from any higher motive. If they do, they will see that a clearing-house, to absorb the money from business, cannot be allowed to exist. In the present condition of affairs, there is no possibility of a revival of business, or that there shall not be a general breaking up of productive employments, and a rapid transfer of property to the money-lenders. The less people try to do business upon the plan in vogue, the longer it will be possible for any considerable portion of them to retain property in their own right. If it was possible to revive business, to be carried on by borrowing money, as it would have to be done if carried on at all, and the effort was backed by all the property in the country, the money-lenders would take it all in a very few years. To show that the operation of depositing money in banks, and disbursing it by cheques and drafts, literally adds the money to the lending capital of the banks; also to show that learned men appear to see nothing wrong in the effect on business and labor of holding money to lend, but, on the contrary, seem to think that it is a commendable operation, I quote from Professor Jevon's chapters on " Book Credit," and " Banking System."

" Considerable economy of the precious metals arises, as we have seen, from passing about pieces of paper representing gold coin, instead of the coin itself. But a far more potent source of economy, is what we may call the Cheque and Clearing System, whereby debts are not so much paid, as balanced off against each other. The germ of the method is to be found in the ordinary practice of *book credit*. If two firms have frequent transactions with each other, alternately buying and selling, it would be an absurd waste of money to settle each debt immediately it arose, when, in a few days, a corresponding debt might arise in the opposite direction. Accordingly, it is the common practice of firms having reciprocal transactions, to debit and credit each other in their books with the debt arising out of each transaction, and only to make a cash payment when the balance happens to become inconveniently great. To represent the highly complex system of book credit which is organized by the bankers of a large kingdom, we shall have to employ a method of diagramatic notation. I will therefore remark that the simplest case or type of book-credit, is represented by the formula

$$P\text{———}Q,$$

Each of the letters, P and Q, indicates a person or a firm, and the line indicates the existence of transactions between them. Only in special cases, however, will this direct balancing of accounts, render the use of cash or of a

7

more complex system unnecessary. Generally speaking, there will be a tendency for a surplus of goods to pass in one direction, so that money must pass in the opposite direction. The manufacturer sells to the wholesale dealer, the latter sells to the retailer, and the retailer to the consumer. By the intervention of the banker, however, the transactions of many different individuals, or even of many branches of trade, are brought to a focus, and a large proportion of payments can be balanced off against each other.

SINGLE BANK SYSTEM.

To obtain a clear notion of the way in which bankers help us to avoid the use of money as the medium of exchange, we must follow up the rise of the system from the simplest case to the complete development of the complex organization now existing in the United Kingdom. Let us imagine, in the first place, that there is an isolated town, having no appreciable dealings with other parts of the world, and possessing only a single bank, in which each inhabitant has deposited all his money. If any person, *a*, then, wishes to make a payment to b, he need not go to his banker, draw out coin, and carry it to b, but may hand to b a cheque requiring the banker to pay the coin to b, if needed. But if b makes payments in the same way, he will not need to draw out any coin. It would be a mere formality for b to receive the coin due from a, and then pay it back over the counter to the credit of his account with the same banker. The payment is made by merely writing the sum of money to the debit of $a's$ account, and to the credit of $b's$ account. If b wishes to make another payment to c, a similar record in the banker's ledger will accomplish the business. However many other traders, $d, e,$ etc., there may be, their mutual transactions may be settled in the same way, without their

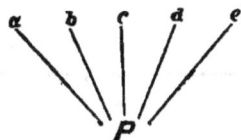

seeing a single coin. We represent this elementary banking organization by the above diagram.

Thus, it is obvious that P represents the

single banker, and *a, b, c, d, e*, his customers.
The deposit banks of Amsterdam and Ham-
burg form perfect illustrations of this arrange-
ment. So long as we regard only the inter-
nal transactions of a town, then a stationary
amount of coin, lying untouched in the bank,
will allow the whole to be accomplished. If
the traders never require to make payments
to a distance, the metallic money might be
dispensed with altogether. But since any of
the customers, *a, b, c*, etc., may want his money,
the banker ought to keep at least as much as
will meet possible demands."

SYSTEM OF TWO BANKS.

"As a second case, let us suppose that there
is a town which is able to support two banks.

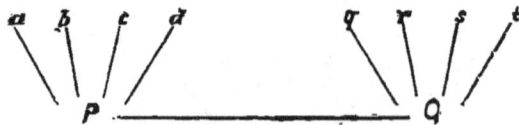

Some of the inhabitants keep their money in
one bank, and some in the other, but all whom
it is requisite to consider, have an account
with one or the other. In the diagram, let P
and Q be the two bankers, *a, b, c, d*, being cus-

tomers of P, and q, r, s, t, customers of Q. Now, the mutual transactions of a, b, c, d, will, as before, be balanced off in the books of P, and similarly with the customers of Q. But if a has to make a payment to q, the operation becomes somewhat more complex. He draws a cheque upon P, and hands it to q, who may, of course, demand coin from P. Not wanting coin, he carries the check to his own banker, Q, and pays it in to his account, in place of coin. It is the banker, Q, who will now have to present the cheque upon P, and it might seem as if the use of coin would be ultimately required. There will be other persons, however, making payments in the town in the same manner, and the probability is very great that some of these will result in giving P cheques upon Q, and some in giving Q cheques upon P. The two bankers, then, will be in the position of the two traders, before described, (p. 251) who have a running account. At the worst the payment to be made in coin, will be only the balance of what is due in opposite directions; but as this balance will probably tend in one direction one day, and in the opposite direction the next day, the balance need only be paid when it assumes inconvenient proportions."

COMPLEX BANK SYSTEM.

" A large commercial town usually possesses several or many banks, each with its distinct body of customers. The mutual transactions of each body will, as before, be balanced off in the books of their common bank, but the larger part of the transactions will now be cross ones, resulting in a claim by one banker upon another. The probability is very great, indeed, that each banker will have to receive, as well as to pay, each day; but it does not follow that he will pay to the same as those who are going to pay to him. The complexity of relations becomes considerable; thus among fourteen banks there are $\frac{14 \times 13}{2}$ or 91 different pairs which may have mutual claims, and among fifty banks there would be no less than 1,225 pairs. The result is, that P might happen to have a considerable balance to pay to Q, and yet might be going to receive about the same sum from R. or S. The actual carrying about of coin, under such circumstances,

would be absurd, because a manifest extension
of the book-credit system at once meets the
difficulty.   The several banks need only agree
to appoint, as it were, a *bankers' bank*, to hold
a portion of the cash of each bank, and then
the mutual indebtedness may be balanced off,
just as when a bank acts for individuals.   In
the figure we see four banks, P, Q, R, S, each
with its own body of customers, but brought
into connection with each other by the bankers' bank, X.

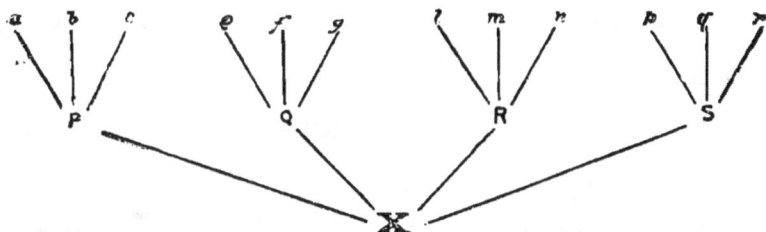

"P need not now send a clerk to present
bundles of cheques upon Q, R, and S, but can
pay them into the central bank, X, where,
after being placed to the credit of P and
sorted out, they will be joined to similar par-
cels of cheques received from Q, R, S, and
finally presented at the banks upon which
they are drawn.   Thus all the payments made
by cheques will be effected without the use of

coin, just as if there were only a single bank in the town. What each bank has to pay each day, will usually be balanced pretty closely by what it has to receive. Such balance as remains will be paid by a transfer in the books of X, the bankers' bank. It is not precisely true that there is in every English town, a bankers' bank, which thus manages the payments between banks. The accountant's part of the work is carried out by an institution called the Clearing-House, managed by a committee of bankers, and the Bank of England is employed to hold the deposits of the bankers, and make transfers which close the transactions of each day."

It has been said that the effect of depositing the money in bank, and using cheques and drafts in business, practically gives the money to the banks to be lending capital; it may be added that the high interest charged soon enables the banks to turn the balance of all accounts in their favor, and the money becomes theirs, in fact.

It is not possible to convey in detail the evils that are inflicted by the few upon the many, by means of taking money out of the use that exists for it, in the business of society, and for which by law and custom of society it is made. For like drawing sap from a tree, the incision and gradual waste of the tree's life may be seen and expressed, but not the hunger and thirst of the decaying tree and its branches, nor the efforts of the ebbing life to staunch the inexorable wound. The wreck of business among the people is easily seen, and may be described, if it was supposed to be useful to do more than call attention to the fact; but what pen could describe the effect upon the minds of the people; of the long years of struggling against fate, to save, first, their business and property; then their business and only a home; then only one of these, to end at last with neither business nor a home, and only the inexorable law of government and society that demands the procuring and employment of money in worldly affairs, remains. Or, as the alternative, to sink out of society, and become a vagrant and pauper. Though the bitter cup of merchandising in money has been forced upon the people with a relentless hand, reflection must convince them that they have but tasted it over the brim; that the cup is full, and that nothing but complete degradation and servitude will drain it. There is no stopping-place or middle-ground. It must either be a right to get money in exchange for property or services, unrestricted by any right to make gain by merchandising in it, with the possibilities of general freedom and elevation of the masses of the people through honorable employments and cultivation, or it must be vassalage of business and the producing millions, and widespread pauperism.

The contest is inaugurated; it cannot be avoided; it must go on as it is going; business and labor to be more and more oppressed and degraded, or the people must revert to first principles. Re-read the Declaration of Independence and the Constitution of the United States, and elect a Congress that will assert and maintain the rights of the whole people in money; which is no less or other than their rights to " life, liberty, and the pursuit of happiness."

CHAPTER XIII.

DEFENDING MONEY-LENDING.

The arguments advanced in defense of money-lending, like those in defense of all other great wrongs, are unworthy of reasoning men. To illustrate this we will cite the arguments that the writer has met with most frequently, in works and discussions on money-lending. It is, " that if there is no consideration to be paid for the use of money, nobody will lend it, and that, as a consequence, a great many could not get money to go into business.

The final conclusions of the above conditions, must strike every one as being false and absurd. If the defenders of the evil had followed up the condition, that if there is no consideration to be paid for the use of money nobody will lend—which, in itself, is true enough—with the same study and care that they manifest in their efforts to defend the money-lenders, they would have been able to picture a condition in the affairs of society unattended with the disorders "with which," in the words of a noted writer, "usury must always be attended."

But instead of this, they try to make it appear, that if no gain can be made by lending money, nobody who had money, would part with it, and that it would be impossible for any person to get it. Now, it is very clear that such a condition of affairs would have exactly the opposite tendency. No one of right mind would hold money if it was bringing him nothing, but was wasting and being taxed away, any longer than he could help; when, by investing it in business and property, he could be making something out of it. If lending money for interest was prohibited, it would not, as some seem to think, interfere, in the least, with any one who could have done so before, engaging in any orderly business.

The conditions under which money ever has been lent—and much more so now—with a few exceptions, are such that any one who could borrow, could obtain the same amount and even more, if the money was, as it should be, only profitable to the holder as he parted with it in exchange for property, or productive labor. For it is clear that under such a condition of affairs, the property that was before required for security could readily be converted into money, as all kinds of property would be sought after for investment. This, also, would cause the regulation of the price of property in the only orderly way, that is, in accordance with the just law of supply and demand. The exceptions referred to above are indeed exceptions. They are those who, by good business qualifications and talent have obtained money to invest in business, through the confidence of friends. Now, again, it is evident that under the above condition of business affairs, such persons would be anything but sufferers from it. There would be a great demand for them to fill honorable positions, and on salaries, too, that would enable them to become partners or independent. And while they would be relieved from the cares and dangers attending business done on borrowed capital, they would be free from the almost inevitable crash and partially-paid creditors that follow the attempt to pay back the money borrowed and invested in business.

CHAPTER XIV.

IMMORAL EFFECTS OF MONEY-LENDING.

The effect of money-lending does not necessarily make men drunkards, thieves, or murderers ; but its effects upon the morals of the people are very bad. When people find their business breaking up, despite their most earnest efforts and frugality, and see upon all sides of them discouragements to the producing classes, while the money-lenders are reaping a rich harvest, they are very apt to feel that the government, in making money, and making it the only legal sign of value and legal tender, and permitting it to be made merchandise of, is a hard master. The loss of respect for the laws, and the thought that they inflict injustice, and that by the injustice, privation and want is forced upon dear and dependent ones, are bad instructors of honesty and morals. If the thoughts have so little scope as not to comprehend the injustice of the monetary laws, that leave the producing masses of the people to become the prey of the money-holders, while there is a consciousness of the increasing poverty of the producers of wealth; and of the idle luxury of the money-lenders, the declension to the conclusion that there is no such thing as justice, will become very easy. This, also, is a bad school for any of the humanizing virtues. While the uninstructed but industrious people are going through these sad experiences, there is nothing in the current literature touching the condition of affairs, that has any tendency to strengthen in the mind the stricken principles of right, or to check a downward tendency. Conscious of having lived lives of severe industry and rigid frugality, and that they and their class are sinking deeper and deeper into poverty, they are told that it is all owing to extravagant living, and to too much production; and that what is needed is to live more economically, and to wait until the surplus production is worked off. Instead of giving support to the wavering and doubting minds, hope is taken from them, and they are left to sink. The degradation of the masses of the people, as the result of the money being taken out of business and held to lend, is no new thing; it existed in all countries where the business prevailed. It reduced the industrious and frugal people of ancient Rome to poverty, and then to the degradation of receiving alms from the public treasuries and storehouses; and it is rapidly making vast numbers of the people of the United States familiar with the same degradation. In midsummer of 1876, it is reported that fifteen hundred people received support from public charity in the city of Columbus, Ohio, besides the inmates of the poor-house. In the Cincinnati Daily *Gazette*, of Thursday, July 27, 1876, under the head of "Bread Riot," it is reported that, " In accordance with a call from some perturbed spirits, the workmen, who could conscientiously call themselves idle and starving, met on the Esplanade yesterday morning, about eight o'clock, as a method of their resentment at the present condition of affairs."

Passing on we find that they went to the city building, where " the assembled toilers were informed that nothing could be done for them at the present. Making the best of the refusal, they distributed themselves as if they were waiting, after the manner of the antique and noble Romans, to have elemosynary corn distributed to them."

Instances of this kind are becoming painfully frequent, and the reports of the breaking up of the long established and useful business of the country are so common, that they have ceased to attract attention. To give further proof of the pitiable condition that the laboring people of the country are reduced to, we insert here from the New York *Herald* of the 23d of August, 1876 :

" WORK OR BREAD.—Much interest is felt by the idle workingmen of Newark, in the issue between the idle workingmen of the metropolis and the authorities, touching the question of supplying work. So it is in Elizabeth and other leading cities of the State. The workingmen of Elizabeth have addressed to the authorities a petition, which is as follows :

' The undersigned, citizens of the city of Elizabeth, and the most of us with families dependent upon us for support, earnestly and
respectfully ask your honorable body to take
some action that will provide us with work.
Should the common council, in their wisdom,
resolve in favor of some public improvements,
the city authorities can give labor to many of
our number, who are now not only out of
work, but actually in want of the necessaries
of life. Hoping our humble petition may be
favorably received, we shall ever pray,' etc.
Accompanying the petition was another from
property-owners, urging that, in the interests
of humanity, the requests of the workingmen
be complied with."

Can anybody doubt the demoralizing tendency of the wrecked, hopeless condition set-
tling down upon the workingmen, the producers of the world's wealth though they are ?

CHAPTER XV.

GENERAL PRINCIPLES.

The question relating to money, like every other question, when looked at from first principles, has just two sides to it ; one is the right side, and the other is the wrong side. Usage and changes may obscure the right, and make it difficult to arrive at conclusions unmixed with wrong, but in its first principles it is not so. When right and wrong have become mixed in any matter of inquiry there is no way to get a view of the truth, but to resolve the question into its original elements, and study the elements in their own light. There has been an effort in this little book to bring up this elementary work and urge its importance, and also in some degree to perform the work of analyzing the questions relating to money. It is supposed that the work performed so far is much in the nature of quarrying blocks of stone that others will cut and polish for themselves; but the work must go on. This question must be presented to everyone stripped of the covering of mystery with which, of late years, it is claimed by many to be surrounded. Mystery is a very suspicious robe for anything that concerns the people. Anything that concerns the people to know is not mysterious. It may be common; lying on the surface of material things and directly effecting the first thoughts of everyone, and therefore easily understood by everyone, as the questions concerning money are; or it may be complex and require closer investigation and higher points of observation, but if it affects the human being it is not mysterious. The term when applied to questions affecting the people has nothing in it but the acknowledgment of ignorance; unless it is a special coinage to cover up falsity and wrong, as is certainly the only use there is for the term in questions connected with money. There is nothing wrong in using the term mystery, if it is understood that it is merely

offered as an acknowledgment of ignorance;
but if it is offered as an end or barrier to
thought and investigation on any subject
affecting the people, it is wrong. Of all things
that affect the affairs of human beings money
is the most common and pervading, and it
controls the worldly interest of every individual. Can anyone believe that if it was not
taken out of its function and wrongfully
applied to another there would be any mystery or even complexity of character or function about it. If there was, that circumstance
alone would prove it to be an enormity, and
that it ought not to exist; for things that are
common, and that affect the life of all, are
easily understood by all, even by those of
ordinary information. What, then, is the
meaning of the mystery that is thrown around
the questions relating to money? The source
from which the claim of mystery comes may
help us to understand why it is raised. If
there was any truth in the application of the
term; if the subject was really complex and
required great scope of thought to understand
it, the first, and, in fact, the only ones, likely

to be perplexed by the question would be the common people, those whose thoughts it is supposed take in but a very small circle. But they never speak of the mysteries of finance or money. The expression never originated with them. If they use it, it is a sure sign that they have been at a political meeting, and have heard candidates for office talk, or that they have been reading political platforms. The common people know that money is wonderfully simple, and that it simplifies everything that it comes in contact with. They know that it is as essential in their worldly affairs as the air is to their bodily life, and that death to business must be the result of depriving it of money, as surely as it is the result of depriving the body of air to breathe. Now, if a number of men should commence business, and, for power, dam up a stream, and thereby fill the air of a populous country with malaria, and one after another of the people were becoming sick and dying, there might be some talk of mystery, and it would be sure to originate with the operators of the unwhole-some business and their friends. If the suffering people had no remedy, or, at least, thought that they had none, they would suffer and die, but they would not talk about it as a mystery.   They might lose respect for their government if it failed to give them relief; and some of them, in the rebellious spirit of Job's wife, might think of cursing God and dying, but they would not stultify common reason and sense by calling it a mystery. The same is true of money.   The common people know that under the laws of the government it is essential to their business, and that if it does not circulate in their business in exchange for that which they have to exchange for it, that is, in exchange for their labor and property, that their business must die.   They may see the bankers and money-lenders holding the money to lend, and refusing to part with it for anything but promises for its return to them with increase, while the business all over the country is reeling to its fall from want of the money, and even feel that their own business is suffering, but they will not call it a mystery until they have listened to the apologizers of the evil business of bank-

ing and money-lending. These invent a new
use for the term, to excuse or conceal the evil.
The common people may be made to think
that there is no remedy, and they will quietly
see their business broken up, and themselves
and families impoverished, and even pauper-
ized; but they will not call it a mystery, and
it is well. The straight-forward common honesty and sense of the people who look at
things and speak about them as they are, is
the one thing that gives hope of the elevation
of the race. It is now the duty of the people to look at this question of money, in the
straight-forward light that it occupies in business affairs.

In the business both of the government and
people, it is necessary to have one authoritative
measure and standard of value and medium of
exchange. Why is this necessary? It is necessary in order that values may be measured and
exchanged in large or small amounts, to suit
every person's circumstances, and that there
may be a medium of communicating the services of each member of society to all, and of
all to each. Money is made to perform these

important functions in the affairs of the government and people, and it does it perfectly
and with the most exact justice and convenience to all, when it circulates among the people, in exchange for their services and usefulness.   This usefulness for which money is exchanged, may consist of services rendered or
of property.   The services and property are
necessary to all in some form or other, and it
might happen, owing to the common need of
the services and property, that people would
not justly and equitably exchange them for
money, if custom and law did not make money
necessary in business, to exchange values and
to pay business balances, taxes, and public
revenues.   The legal character that is given
to money, makes it a most equitable medium
of performing the high offices just enumerated, in the affairs of the government and the
people.   But how does it do it?   Let us look
at the operation.   It does it because it is
necessary in business for the people to get it
to measure the value of everything, according to a law called the law of supply and demand, and pass it from one person to another

in exchange for the things valued, so that any
one may get money at the correct value of his
property or services, and by means of it be
placed in a condition to procure the things
that he may stand in need of. As money is
made of gold and silver, or of paper in quantities agreeing in supply with gold and silver,
it will be reasonably uniform and just, and
will operate for every person alike. That is
reasonable, and there is no mystery about it.
But suppose the money is allowed to become
private merchandise, and that the holders are
allowed to make gain, by charging for the use
of it, while by notes and promises to pay
money, they hold it bound to return to them,
out of the business that it was made for; how
will that operate on the affairs of the people?

Let Congressmen answer that question.
They will have to answer it reasonably, and
show by the answer that they are ready to
make laws that will do justice to all, or they
must cease to be Congressmen. In the meantime it will be seen that such a condition
would open the door, and by pecuniary inducement, unlimited in amount would invite

those who at the time might be in possession of the money, to perpetrate the most cruel wrong upon all other people. The effect would be cruel beyond measure upon the producers; it is the products of labor, and consequently labor, also, that are the principal subjects controlled by the money measure. Everything that operates to prevent or retard equitable and just exchange of money for property and labor, is borne directly, and to the remotest consequences, by the producers. Not only is all the interest paid by them, but, as has been shown before, all the consequences of the waste of the time of the money in making return movements to the money-lenders, and the breaking of business connections effected by taking the money out of business to make the return, and from continually declining values, and consequent discouragement of exchanging money for labor and property. In short, money-lending is robbery of the producing classes; and it has nothing in itself to cure the evil it works, but goes on with increasing momentum till it is prevented by law; or, until it works revolution of government.

The work of stopping, and hereafter pre-
venting the great evil, is for the people. Justice to all makes this work their duty. Although it is nothing but the common principle
of right and justice towards all, the argument
in the present conditions will necessarily be
addressed to the matter of protecting the utterly exposed rights and freedom of the producing classes.

The framers of the Constitution of the
United States have made it easy work for the
people to procure and maintain their rights in
the money. For they provided in that important instrument that " Congress shall have
the right to coin money and to regulate the
value thereof, and of foreign coins." No one,
whose opinion will have any weight, will pre-
tend that any other power, or that any person,
can justly claim a right to put a value on
money, by any rule not fixed and regulated by
Congress; or deny that Congress may, by
fines and forfeitures and confiscations, maintain its regulations of the value of money.
All, therefore, that the people have to do, is
to unite in the election of a Congress that

will repeal all bank charters and privileges, that allow making merchandise of money; and that will enact a law prohibiting the taking of interest or gain, on any form of promise to pay money, except the promises of the United States, with forfeiture to the United States government of all money and property involved in violating the law. This will cause the money to seek the channels of business for which it is made, a condition that will at once restore the broken business of the country, to be no more disturbed by panics. It will also restore to all of the people, rich and poor, their common rights in the money, and neither more nor less, a boon that the producers of the world's wealth have not enjoyed since the fall of Adam.

After more than four years of active interchange of thought, with people of various business and professions, it is believed that the people will be almost unanimous in favor of such action, as soon as there is presented anything like a reasonable statement of the general rights in money. It is hoped that this book may prove sufficient for the purpose, and afford substantial footing to maintain the rights of the whole people, in this their most important concernment. The business of lending money for interest, has no rational or just ground to stand upon, and it must go down ; though the arguments used against it may be only like rough, undressed stones from the quarry.

It is not supposed it will be necessary to disturb party lines, as there will be a vast majority of both parties in favor of it. Those occupying positions of preferment in the parties, will not be likely to be the first to move in the matter. It would be strange if they did. Their places of preferment being given to them on old grounds, it is not to be expected that they will make the first movement on new questions. But the people cannot afford to wait for those who, on account of circumstances that have no relation to the question at issue, will move slowly in it. The tendency to adhere to established thought and practice, operates with peculiar force with those known as the learned. Their learning, acquired through years of application to

books and authorities, is not favorable ground
for thoughts that are new, and require the establishing of new orders; especially if it is to
bring up the plain and unfashionable, and to
disturb the influential. There is nothing in
favor of this plain principle of justice to the
laboring millions found in their learning, but
every unreasonable thing on the other side;
and they will be most of all likely to let it
alone. They will be slow to attack the principle of the common rights of the people in
money, relieved of the right of private merchandise in it, when they come to consider it
fairly, but it is not found in their books, and
they must not be expected to take kindly to
it at first. The public press was founded on
different ideas, and it must not be looked to
to lead off on this entirely new principle. But
it also will not lift a type to oppose it. The
work, then, is left entirely to the people. Their
condition, as well as the condition of their descendants, depends upon their taking up the
work, and performing it thoroughly. Organ-
ize in your school districts, townships, counties, and congressional districts; and send

men to Congress to do the work. The learned may attack the style of this book. They
may also attack the way in which the people
go about the work of accomplishing the reform. And it will be well for all to remem-
ber, that the evil they are about to reform is
an old one; and that those who are engaged
in banking and money-lending, have only
shown themselves wise in the things of mam-
mon, by going into the business, and not waiting until others took the start of them. The
people must make the laws of the government
right on the subject of making gain on money,
while it is held as private merchandise, before
they ask the holders of it to let it go in exchange for property, or in business, and they
will find all the better class of the money-
lenders will operate with them.

TITLE OF THE BOOK.

The rights of the people in money is the
title of this little volume. The title was
adopted as expressing the result that the book
is written to promote.

In the latter part of the year 1871 the
writer was watching the currents of business,

and trying to trace their sources and tendencies, and he saw that the bankers and money-lenders were driving the money out of regular business into channels of speculation. That people were getting restive in regular business, and were seeking positions from which results could be reached quickly.

The cause of this was discovered to be in tne fact that the money was controled by bankers and money-lenders, who compelled it to return periodically out of business to themselves; and that, as a result, all of what might be called the regular but slow-moving productive business of the country was quite out of its reckoning and was getting into shoal water, where sailing was rough.

So far, matters were seen pretty clearly, and also that it was a duty to work for a cure of the evil. That work was taken up at once, first in efforts to get those who were competent to bring it before the world by speaking and writing, to engage in the work. Failing there, then in trying to get prominent officers of the government and members of Congress, to take up the work of stopping merchandising in money.

Not succeeding with men in office, the art of writing newspaper articles was tried, and always succeeded in getting hints that the articles were not needed. Everything else failing, it was determined to write a book. This little volume is the result. If it is at all important that the people should know their rights in money, a book to promote the object is needed. The publication of the title of the book developes the fact that there is a very general lack of thought and information on the subject of the common rights of the people in money. Intelligent men, candidates for Congress, discuss the question of finance as a question that capital, by which they mean money, and business, by which they mean trade, are interested in; but without the least discernable thought that labor has any rights in money or finance until the labor is turned into money. They show the people truly that they have an interest in money; that when they have gotten it for their labor they have an interest in the money having the highest possible value in it. That, in such case, it is their interest that the money should be gold or be at par with gold.

Labor may be said to produce or renew the wealth of the world every year. Money is made to measure the value of the production or labor, and by a fair and just exchange of money for it to make just return for the labor or production. The rights of labor in money are, that the exchange of money for labor, and for property, the product of labor, shall proceed on fair and equal terms. That this fair and equal exchange may take place, it is manifest that the holders of the money must not be allowed to make gain out of it while they hold it back from such exchange; nor while, by notes or promises to pay money, they hold it bound to return to themselves. If the holders of the money are allowed to make gain out of it while they refuse to exchange it for property or labor, it is evident that the exchange of money for the produced wealth cannot go on till the price of the property or labor falls sufficiently to compensate for the charge on the money, and also to afford sufficient allowance for the unmeasurable disasters that merchandising in money is known to bring upon trade. The rights of labor in money just referred to, are the rights of labor performed, but if these rights are violated, it is evident that the effect will be projected with intensified evil upon the labor to be performed. The increase of the evil comes from diminished employment as well as constantly falling prices of labor. Besides the important rights in money referred to, the laborers have the rights of the money-holders in the money they get. They have the right that the money shall be a true and, as nearly as may be, an unvariable measure of value and medium of exchange. But this right of the producers of wealth is as one drop of water to a bucketfull when compared to their right that money shall enter business in exchange for labor or property, without gain to a holder, or charge for the use of it, while, by notes or promises to pay money it is bound to return to a lender. The discussion of money or finance, as it is conducted by statesmen and writers on political economy in this age, involves questions merely of money and trade.

The money-lender, claiming and exercising
the right of merchandise in the money he
holds, turns it into such channels as will realize
for him the best profits by way of interest, and
will allow him at short periods to recover
possession of the money. Business, or trade
in labor and property, finds itself unable to
compete with the demands the money-lenders
make or find for the money, and trade wants
a change.

Here the argument, not to say chaos, com-
mences between trade and money. The
money-lenders admit that trade, or business
as it is called, cannot compete for the money,
and they say the reason is, that everything is
inflated by the superabundance of money issued during the war of the rebellion, and that
the remedy for existing evils is to be found in
a reduction of the prices of labor and resultant
property to a gold standard. As might be
expected, they ignore the rights of the people
in money. Political economists are not slow
to confirm their position, and claim a reduction of the cost of production as the way to
restore trade.

Statesmen, liking the respectable company
of learned writers and money-lenders, think
they are about right, though some times, with
a gentle inclination towards the people, venture the remark that " the subject of money
and finance is a very deep subject, a little too
deep for them." But among them all, though
the money is made to measure and transfer
the wealth of the world from the producers of
it to the consumers of it, no where is recog-
nized the common rights of the producers in
the money. With them all it is a question to
be adjusted between the traders in labor and
property and the money-holders. Though
the rights of producers be still ignored, it will
be impossible to adjust the contest between
the traders and money-lenders on the terms
the lenders do, and will always make for the
money until they are controlled by government, as has been sufficiently shown in these
pages. The rights of the producers that
money shall cease to be an article of private
merchandise, is so clear and important, and
the way to secure the right through Congressional regulation of the value of money is so

safe and easy, that the subject is commended
with confidence to the care of the producers,
with the remarks that it is the producers who
pay all the interest and charges on money,
and not the traders in their labor, or in property, the products of their labor.

The investigation of the subject that pre-
ceded the writing of the rights of the people
in money, convinced the writer, as stated else-
where in the book, that the reform of the great
evil the producers are suffering through banking and money-lending must spring from the
producers themselves; but the entire ignoring
of their rights in money was not fully realized
till the publication of the title of the book
caused it to appear. If they are not yet fully
convinced of the necessity of vigorously com-
mencing the work of reforming the evil, they
soon will be, for the evil will not weaken or
cure itself.

They need not be discouraged because the
learned do not lead off in the reform. Common reflection, with the rough cast arguments
they may find in this volume, will make them
more than a match for any sophistry that may

be offered against their common rights in money.

EXTRAVAGANT LIVING.

The universally acknowledged disorder that is existing in the business affairs of the people of the United States, and which has existed in a most tangible form for a number of years, is generally accounted for by people in easy circumstances as the result of extravagant living. The cool manner in which well-off people account for their neighbors' adverse worldly circumstances as the result of extravagant living, while they themselves live daily at an expense that these same neighbors never venture upon, even for a holiday, would be a worthy subject of study for the curious.

The subject would not be the less suggestive that these philosophers would generally be found to be holding money bound to return out of business to them, with large increase, under forfeiture of five or six for one. The form that the disorders of the country is generally seen under, is that of unconsumed production—production that is not and cannot be bought and consumed; and from this cause factories and other sources of extensive production are compelled to stop or contract operations. These stoppages and contractions of productive employments tend to throw large numbers of the people out of work, and as a consequence the world is becoming filled with idleness, dissipation and pauperism. Men with families to house, clothe and feed, go through the discouraging experience of finding themselves thrown out of employment, and through every effort they are capable of making, they sink deeper and deeper into poverty, till they are compelled to accept public charity, and become acknowledged paupers.

Now, when Job's three friends heard of all this evil that was come upon him, they came every one from his own place: Eliphaz, the Temanite, and Bildad, the Shuhite, and Zophar, the Naamathite; for they had made an appointment together to come to mourn with him, and to comfort him."

The record goes on to indicate that Job's friends proved to be "miserable comforters;" but their words do not appear at very great disadvantage, either as to reason or intention, when compared with the comforters who philosophically inform the poorly-housed, half-clothed and half-starved victims of the present derangement in business, "that they are, and have been, living too extravagantly." These comforters claim that the evil is the result of over-production, stimulated by inflated money, and extravagant living, stimulated into life by the same cause. Now, extravagant living means extravagant consumption. If there was any general extravagance in living the superabundant produce would rapidly disappear; in fact, a redundancy of production would never appear in the home labor of an extravagant-living people, for the two very potent reasons: first, that the extravagant living would consume the production, and second, that extravagant livers never prove to be superabundant producers.

Another phase of these men's philosophy is, that there are too many trying to live by speculation, to the neglect of regular, productive employment. This would be a great evil, and no doubt it exists to an unhealthy de-

gree, and it results from the evil business of
money-lending, but the over-production which
is said to be the cause of the stagnation in
business, certainly could not spring from people speculating, to the neglect of productive
labor. It is very evident the Temanite, the
Shuhite, and the Naamathite of the present
time, are as much of failures, as their archi-
types were in Job's time.

I never borrowed money, and consequently
I never paid any interest. These were the
remarks made by an industrious day laborer,
on hearing the title and some of the principles of the book entitled " The Rights of the
People in Money " discussed. The subject
being taken up and examined, it was found
that in the three years of 1868, 1869 and 1870,
he had performed an average of two hundred
and seventy days work for every year; and
that his average wages had been one dollar
and seventy-five cents per day, which made of
wages for every year, four hundred and sev-
enty-two dollars and fifty cents. While in the
years 1873, 1874 and 1875, by his greatest
efforts to get employment, he was employed

one hundred and seventy days per year, at an average wages of one dollar and twenty-five cents per day, or two hundred and two dollars and fifty cents for every year; a difference of two hundred and seventy dollars against every year of the last decade, or a difference of eight hundred and ten dollars in three years. By the best data furnished, it was thought that in the last decade, there had been an average saving in prices paid for articles of food and clothing consumed, of about twenty dollars for every year, or sixty dollars for the three years; leaving a total loss in three years of seven hundred and fifty dollars, or just two hundred and fifty dollars per year, while he· admits that the year 1876, half gone, promises to be worse in results than any of the other years.

This man is known to stand at the very head of that very large and useful class of men known as day laborers. Yet it is evident he is standing upon the very brink of pauperism, and unless the oppression is removed from the labor of the country, he must soon join that large and constantly increasing throng, that have been compelled to receive public support. The productive labor of the country pays all the interest and charges upon money, whether the laborers do, or do not, borrow; for, as said before on this subject, those who borrow money for business, do not pay the interest. The world might be challenged in vain to show any true reason for rejecting the conclusion that the day laborer instanced, paid a portion of all the interest collected upon the money of the country, that bore the same relation to the whole interest paid, that his labor bore to the whole labor of the country.

The labor pays all the interest collected upon money. The portion that may be left of the products of the labor, for the use and benefit of the laborers, depends upon the circumstances under which the labor may be performed. In the years 1868, 1869 and 1870, there was still some portion of the money that had been paid by the government to the people, for war services and material, passing into circulation. This money supported business through those years, and labor received employment and reasonable support during that time. That money was exhausted by the year 1873, and the business of the country had to depend in the years 1873, 1874 and 1875, as it does now, continually upon money borrowed. Labor, under the first circumstances, had a margin left, that it was possible for the laborer to live upon, but not to live extravagantly, as every person of sense knows; while it is not possible for the laborers, under the circumstances of the last decade of years named, nor at the present time, to live the lives of free citizens. It is impossible but that under the existing circumstances of labor and business, a very large portion of that useful class of laborers known as day laborers, will fall into a condition to require public support.

In saying that the laborer pays all the interest that may be collected on money used in the business of a country, it is not intended to deny that circumstances may occasionally cause the consumers of the products of labor to bear a part of the burden; such circumstances as grow out of war, might cause it for a short time. But no circumstances will, for any considerable time together, relieve the laborer from bearing the whole weight of the interest collected upon the money that may be used, as the measure of value and medium of exchange, whatever the interest may be. The bankers and money-lenders of the United States, are a much more onerous burden upon the people, than would be a large class of political aristocracy, sustained by revenues assessed upon the people.

The burden of taxes and revenues collected from the people, is borne by them severally, according to their ability, and though the collections be large, a political aristocracy returns the money to the people, for services, and property, the products of their labor.

A political aristocracy, sustained by rents or revenues, collected by any just rule, would be a light burden upon the people, as compared to the bankers and money-lenders of the United States. A political aristocracy control no money but their rents and revenues, and this they return, as just stated, to the people, in a way that aids and stimulates labor ; whereas, the bankers and money-lenders, while they collect as largely from the people as a political aristocracy, they control the whole money in a way that cannot fail to break up business and labor, and continually lessen the ability of the people to pay.

This book started with the declaration that the bankers and money-lenders are rapidly breaking up the business of the country, are taking the property from the masses of the people, and reducing them to a condition of hopeless poverty and degradation. It is generally admitted that the condition described is spreading rapidly over the people. The writer charges the unjust control of the money as a lending capital, with producing the condition. Learned writers on political economy and statesmen, charge it to over-production, extravagant living, and speculating, to the neglect of productive industry; all these evils, as they say, resulting from inflated paper money. The writer is no advocate of inflated money, but denies that inflation, of itself, has any tendency to produce the existing condition. He charges the political writers and statesmen with perpetrating egregious folly,

10

in ascribing the condition to over-production, extravagant living, and to the people speculating, to the neglect of productive labor; and in claiming that these result, as a natural consequence, from inflated money. The writer is willing to admit that this hasty handling of the subject, cannot prove to be equal to its importance, but he confidently trusts the positions he has taken, to the scrutiny of a discerning public.

QUESTIONS ANSWERED.

Now that the neighbors know that the writer is getting out a book against lending money for interest, the question is often asked him, sometimes with apparent concern: How the people will get money? Sometimes the question is accompanied with remarks that direct the mind to the point of transition from the present condition, where it is expected the needed money may be borrowed, to the proposed order where the money would be expected only through business channels in exchange for property or services. At other times the question is very clearly directed to the difficulty that people without capital would experience in going into business, if the business of lending money for interest was done away with.

In reference to the first point, namely, how the people would be able to get money necessary to pay taxes and carry on business, while the country would be in the transition state, we might remark, that while it would be very important for a patient suffering from a carbuncle, appearing on the head, that the physician called should understand the malady, and not mistake the swelling for a phrenological development of the neighboring organs of the mind, it might not be desirable that he should follow the exact order of remedy found in the books. It might be very important for the patient, that with a clear and comprehensive understanding of that particular case, the physician should conform the treatment to the case. So it is with the present business malady of the world; it is very important for the patient that the true nature of the disease should be understood by those who may be called to administer remedies. It is of the greatest moment that they should have a clear comprehension of the disease, and of the constitution of the patient; and the nature and effects of remedies applied to business diseases. But it is not necessary that they should find the exact form of remedy laid down in a book.

It is very clear that they will have to bring in the aid of the surgeon, and amputate all the present authorized and unauthorized forms of making gain by making merchandise of money; but the exact kind of stimulant that may be needed, if any, to keep up the vigor of the patient, during the operation, will be best understood and applied by the skillful surgeon at the time of the operation. It might prove to be right for the government when it was breaking up the present outrageous system of money control, to issue small sums of its own paper money to the people, by loans, at the same rate of interest the government pays upon its bonds.

These loans to be secured by the pledge of at least twice the value of unencumbered productive real estate; and to be paid back in three equal parts, at three, six, and nine years.

The issues to be limited to such amount as would agree with a gold standard of money. Thus gold might reasonably be expected to take the place of the paper money as it would be called in.

But these things could be judged of best at the time. First, let the nature of that disease that is to-day filling the world with idleness, and its resulting dissipation, vice, and pauperism, be well understood, and we need not fear but that true remedies can be comprehended and applied to the curing of any and every phase of evil that the malady may develop. In answer to that form of the question that has reference to those who, without capital, might desire to borrow money to go into business, it may be suggested that going into business without capital is itself a disorder that is not to be encouraged. Persons that are qualified to carry on a regular business, would never undertake to do it on money borrowed on promises for the return of the money at set times to the lenders. They know that to effect a return of the money out of any regular business, at set times, would break up the business. If those who desire the business of money-lending to be perpetuated as a means of enabling people without capital to go into business were understood, it would be found that it was not business but speculation they want.

They may be in a somewhat similar state of mind with poor people surrounded with slavery. Though it be the pregnant source of their poverty and degradation, they still support it, it may be with the secret hope that some time they will own slaves. There may be in the mind of the advocate of the business of lending money for interest, a fond looking to a time in the future, a future so full of promise to some people, when they will be money-lenders. It is surely this, or speculation, that they see. It is not conceivable that people of ordinary intelligence would seriously entertain the supposition that any of the regular productive employments followed among men, could be sustained and carried on with money borrowed, and to be returned periodically to the lenders, with increase. It is stated on what appears to be true data, that there are mortgages on real estate in the city of New York, to secure the payment of money to the amount of five hundred millions of dollars. It is not probable that the indebtedness by mortgages is more than half as much as the indebtedness on other securities owed by the people of the city of New York, including the city debt, and their equal portion of the state and county indebtedness. From this it would appear that the population of the city of New York owe fully fifteen hundred million dollars, exclusive of the share which they bear in the indebtedness of the United States government.

There is no reason to suppose that the people of the city of New York owe any more than other portions of the people of the United States, and hence the conclusion is, that the people of the United States owe fully sixty billions of dollars, besides the debt that the United States government owes. Now this vast debt is owed to bankers and money-lenders, whose control of the indebtedness and the accruing interest, operates to turn all money out of, and from productive business,

only for short, disconnected periods as it may
be borrowed of them, on promises for its return to them with increase.   If the interest
upon this indebtedness amounts to an average
rate of ten per cent., it amounts annually to
about forty-eight hundred million dollars.
Though there is not claimed perfect accuracy
for the foregoing calculations, it is believed it
is not too high, either as to the amount of the
debt, or the rate of interest that is actually
charged.

The debt has been created through and by
means of controlling the money that the people are compelled to have in their business,
and to pay their taxes, as a lending capital.
It is not possible but that such control of the
money of business, would result in involving
the people in irredeemable debt, and in the
final overthrow of business ; the transfer of
the property to the money-controllers, and the
degradation of labor.   Nor is it possible that
the evil will cure itself.   Now, if the physi-
cians having the patient in charge, should mistake the carbuncle for a diseased phrenological development ; to be cured, or neutralized,

by cultivating the less vigorously developed organs, the imagination, for instance, to the point of believing that there is " nothing wrong, but a temporary loss of confidence," aided by "a general extravagance of living, and over-production ;" that will work its own remedy through depletion of the patient ; it may go hard with the world, now a very sick patient. To bring the true remedy for the business evils resting upon the world to notice, the writer has used every opportunity that came before him for over four years, and since he became fully satisfied as to the true nature of the malady. It was only after every other means of having it brought before the people failed, that he thought of writing a book. The work has been performed in too much of a hurry, but if it brings the matter to the understanding of the readers, as well as conversations appeared to do for the hearers, it will be entirely successful in bringing the people to a correct understanding of the evil, and the remedy, as far as it may get circulation and a reading. For I can say in truth, that expressions of sentiment by many hundreds of people, after the subject was presented to them, showed a unanimity of understanding and favor of the common rights of the people in money as presented, that never was seen by the writer on any other subject.

CHAPTER XVI.

POLITICAL PARTIES.

Politicians do what they are promoted to do ; but they are the slowest of men to do, or to acknowledge the necessity of new things. This is as it should be. It leaves to the people to project and urge the advances they desire to be made. The present political parties were formed on the slavery question, as it existed in the United States before the rebellion. The parties presented the opportunity to the people to take sides freely on the question ; while an overruling Providence protected the nation in its passage through the " Red Sea." The leaders of the parties are able to go no further. If they are not directed, they will not fail to make and seek dead images to lead them, and to attract the attention of the people. The people must come forward now, not with offerings for the dead images, but with instruction on living questions. The Republican party, claiming to be a progressive party, ought to be able to make a forward movement easily ; and the Democratic party would naturally be willing to quit, or close the book of its dead past. But these rational movements will not be inaugurated by the leaders of the parties. The people must come to the front, and instruct their politicians, not in general terms in vogue at the present time. It is the silliest talk—if it is no worse—to say that we must have a pure administration, a breaking up of rings, honesty in the offices ; and that these things must be secured by electing pure, honest, and candid men to office. It is folly for the people to indulge in such babbling. All men claim to want these things ; and it is the cheapest capital in the trade of parties and candidates, to claim to be the peculiar champions of these virtues ; while the truth is, it is possible for but very few of the people to be acquainted with the candidates for office, and to know whether they are, or are not, honest men.   A politician or party that makes a charge of corruption and fraud, in general terms, and makes or implies promises of their own pre-eminent virtues, ought to be set aside as a dangerous character.   It is a public wrong, that ought to receive the reprimand of public indignation, for a person to make or insinuate, in a general way, charges of fraud or corruption against public men.   Any person of ordinary information, if he is honest, will not do it.   An honest person is slow, in very plain cases of wrong, to charge another with intentional dishonesty, much less to charge or insinuate it, on suspicion or rumor. The crime of slandering men in office is becoming so general, that if it is not stopped, honorable men will cease to take office, and the people will be compelled to take the services in the public offices, of the dishonesty that they have been charging and looking for in the offices.   The people must come forward now ; not to say that times are hard, and that they look to their parties to better them, but they must say exactly what they want done, and how they want it done.   The evil of money-lending has existed, to a greater or less extent, in all countries, and has degraded the many through poverty, and debauched the few through wealth ; and it has assumed proportions in our country that challenge immediate attention. The money that has been received in an orderly way, that is, in exchange for labor and property, has been retired from business, and is held to lend. The need of it in business, and to pay taxes, has compelled people to borrow and to re-borrow it, and to pay, and promise to pay it back with interest, until a debt has accumulated against the producing classes that is overwhelming, and with the interest constantly augmenting, constitutes a sum that cannot be paid, but by the transfer of the property to the money-lender.

IF ARBITRARY DISTINCTIONS IN SOCIETY ARE WRONG,

then are all things wrong that lead to the formation of such distinctions. In the ages that " might assumed to make right," class was an inevitable condition among men. The establishing by government of noble classes, founded upon the display of some pre-eminent public virtue, thereby laying a foundation for the sentiment that virtue is noble, and that nobles were prominent public servants, was a great blessing to mankind. The founders of the government of the United States denied the principle that " might makes right," but claimed human rights, as an inalienable gift from the Creator. This principle they maintained through war, and bequeathed it in the Constitution, to the people of the United States. The people of the United States have, therefore, a right, and it is their duty to attack and overthrow public wrongs, by the exercise of the rights secured to them in the Constitution, when these wrongs have become of general concernment. The wrong of money-lending, at this time pressing with crushing weight upon the industrious millions, has descended, like nearly all other wrongs, through long ages. Although it has nothing but injustice and wrong in it, and wherever it has been practiced, it has marked its course with oppression, and fostered vice among its successful votaries; yet it has always succeeded in making itself acceptable to the learned and influential. In former ages, as may be seen in Montesquieu's " Spirit of Laws," where he speaks of money-lending among the Roman people, when the oppression became unendurable, and before all spirit was crushed out of the people, they, through riot and violence, compelled their government to make some show of correcting the evil. But it was never attacked upon the true ground—that of its utter wrong against the rights of all the people in money. That is, their right to meet the thing that society and the government declares to be money, in their worldly affairs, without any right in the holders to make gain on it, while they refuse to exchange it for labor and property, and hold it bound by notes and promises to pay, to be returned to themselves. Common sense teaches that if the government makes money, and makes it necessary to the people in their worldly affairs, to pay business balances and public revenues, and the holders of it are allowed to make gain, while they refuse to part with it in exchange for labor and property, they will break up the business of the masses of the people, by means of the money, and take their property. But, plain as the principle is, from some cause or other, the oppression has been exercised through all ages ; while the utter injustice of taking interest for money, has been declared or referred to in no instance that the writer is acquainted with, outside of the Word of God. The suffering of the people, their struggles against money-lending, called capital, their degradation, the debauchery of the moneyed few, and from all these causes, the final overthrow of governments, are freely treated of in the pages of history. But it is left for the people of the United States, on their own behalf, under the clear sanction of the Word of God, and their rights under the Constitution, and as free and reasoning men, to deny and overthrow the practice of private merchandising in money.

As this treatise is written by a very plain person, for plain people, it is consistent to still further illustrate the principles of money by a re-statement of them, although the principles have been already stated several times under various forms and in various connec-

11

tions. Money is a necessity in business affairs, as a means of expressing and exchanging values. Gold and silver are the most appropriate materials to make money of; as they are metals that are but little subject to rust; and exist in such limited supply as would render the procuring of them no more remunerative than other useful employments. Gold and silver may be said to be the natural foundation for money.

When society and government make money on a gold and silver basis, and make it necessary to every member of society, by making it the only legal sign of value and legal tender in paying business balances and taxes, money becomes to everyone the most important material thing, and to get money becomes the most important question affecting the natural life. It is not the temporary use of money that becomes necessary to the people by the custom of society, and by the law of the government, but the money itself; for when they pay it out, the only way they have of getting it back is to exchange services or property for it. The constantly recurring need cannot be supplied by borrowing the money on promise to pay it back with increase. Money borrowed, to be paid back at times and with increase set to suit the gain of the lender, would not support the most economical government that has ever been known to exist among civilized men ; and it will not support the individual members of society. Let government show an example of carrying on its affairs with borrowed money and cease to collect revenue, before it asks the people to do the like. When the holders of the money are allowed to make gain by charging for the use of it, and hold it bound to be returned to themselves—and they have extended the operation many times over the amount of the money in the country—it places the people very nearly in the condition that the government would occupy if it ceased to collect revenue and depended upon borrowing money to carry on its affairs.

The private revenue or money, that is required to support the affairs of the members of society, must be derived from their business in exchange for property or services.

But when the holders of the money refuse to let it circulate in exchange for labor and property, they cut off the revenue; and it is impossible for the people to stand, as it would be for a government to survive without revenue. The circumstance that government collects revenue from the money-holders, and pays it out to the people for property and services, and that the money-holders themselves pay out some money for property and labor, modifies the condition for the people, and enables them to continue the struggle for an existence longer than a government could without revenue. Though the end is postponed by these things it cannot be averted. Through increasing hardships for the producing classes, the business of money-lending will move on towards the final overthrow of business and free labor, and the absorption of all the property by the money-lenders.

The proposition by the Greenback party, for the government to offer to the money-lenders government bonds bearing interest at the rate of 3.65 per cent. per annum, and to return the money again on the bonds at the option of the holder, would be the boldest outrage upon the rights of the producing classes that could be devised. The mere matter of having the money where it would be kept safely in times of depressed business and shrinking prices, and returnable at the will of the holder, would cause all the money to disappear from circulation in a very short time. But to add to the inducement a rate of gain that is greater, no doubt than the average net profits of business, what possible inducement would remain to exchange money for labor or property? That such a proposition finds advocates shows the bewildered condition of the people on the subject; and shows the imperative necessity of reverting to first principles, and establishing the true bearings of the question. As already said, this work the people must do. Politicians and the learned men of the world have their faces turned from it—a sure sign that the people and their interests have ceased to furnish impulses in the control of affairs. Let the principle be henceforth insisted upon, that money shall be established on a gold and silver basis, and that the whole people have a right, and shall have the privilege, to meet money in business affairs, without any possible gain being made out of it by dealing in promises to pay money, excepting upon the bonds oi the United States.

The proposition suggests A RADICAL CHANGE —but it will be a just and healthy change, that will disturb no private or public right. It will stop the business of money-lending for gain; but no person can have a right to make gain by setting a value on money when the people choose to prevent it; for the Constitution gives to Congress the right "to coin money and to regulate the value thereof and of foreign coin." It would prevent States from borrowing money, and from authorizing counties, cities, townships, and school-districts to borrow on their bonds, or bills of credit. But, under the Constitution, the States have no right to emit bills of credit; and of course they cannot authorize counties, cities, townships, or school-districts to issue them. But they will suffer no inconvenience, for they can accomplish all desirable measures through taxation, and will not thereby disturb the rights of the productive business of the country in the money.

ERRATA.

Page 141, first line, read " sixty-two " instead of " seventy."

Page 152, sixth line, read " sixty " instead of " forty-eight."

www.ingramcontent.com/pod-product-compliance
Lightning Source LLC
Chambersburg PA
CBHW020547270326
41927CB00006B/750